Understanding Digital Racism

Understanding Digital Racism

Networks, Algorithms, Scale

Sanjay Sharma

ROWMAN & LITTLEFIELD
Lanham • Boulder • New York • London

Credits and acknowledgments for material borrowed from other sources, and reproduced with permission, appear on the appropriate pages within the text.

Published by Rowman & Littlefield
An imprint of The Rowman & Littlefield Publishing Group, Inc.
4501 Forbes Boulevard, Suite 200, Lanham, Maryland 20706
www.rowman.com

6 Tinworth Street, London SE11 5AL, United Kingdom

British Library Cataloguing in Publication Information Available

Library of Congress Cataloging-in-Publication Data Available

Library of Congress Control Number: 2023946901

978-1-78661-393-6 (cloth)
978-1-78661-394-3 (paperback)
978-1-78661-395-0 (electronic)

To Zahra & Nirmal – for a better world

Contents

Acknowledgements

Writing a book about digital media and technology can feel like trying (and failing) to keep pace with a runaway world. This book took longer to write than planned – the impact of Coronavirus, home-schooling, changing jobs and cities all played a part in scrambling best-laid plans. Having said that, studying digital racism over an extended period of time, enabled me to reflect on the underlying, systemic features of a mutating phenomenon.

This book was written while I worked at the Department of Sociology & Communications, Brunel University London, and currently at the Centre for Interdisciplinary Methods (CIM), University of Warwick. I thank my colleagues for their support. And also to the Ada Lovelace Institute, BLAST Fest and British Sociological Association (BSA) Digital Sociology for providing critical spaces to think in.

My project took shape through sharing and discussing perspectives about why it's so challenging to address forms of digital racism. I'd like to thank the following people who were part of these conversations, via personal communications, seminars, workshops, conferences, and invitations to speak and write: Les Back, Maria Puig de la Bellacasa, Phil Brooker, Michael Castelle, Robert Clarke, Carlos Cámara-Menoyo, Jessie Daniels, Monica Degen, Michael Dieter, Nadine El-Enany, David Theo Goldberg, Lesley Henderson, Malcolm James, Helen Kennedy, Adi Kuntsman, Alana Lentin, Celia Lury, Sarita Malik, Shaka McGlotten, Dan McQuillan, Goldie Osuri, Dimitris Papadopoulus, Richard Rogers, Abdullah Safir, Eugenia Sapiera, David Skinner, Nicholas Thoborn, Nate Tkacz, Emma Uprichard and Sivamohan Valluvan.

I express my gratitude to those who supported me in different ways and/or allowed me to sound out copious (inchoate) ideas: Paul Bingley, Virinder

Kalra, Koen Leurs, Noortje Marres, Mal Minhas, Dhiraj Murthy, Anamik Saha, Anita Shervington and Gavin Titley.

Jas Nijjar has been a co-collaborator and invaluable for keeping it conceptual and real. *Part II Algorithms* draws on some material co-authored with him from our article, 'The Post-Racial Politics of Pre-emption', *European Journal of Cultural Studies*, 2023.

My brother, Ash, has always been there to keep me on track. And to the wider Sharma and Puwar families for their kindness. I couldn't have completed this project without the encouragement, support and love from my daughter Zahra, and partner Nirmal.

The writing of this book has been assisted by a Leverhulme Fellowship Award (2019-20) *The Ecology of Digital Racism* (RF-2019-578\8).

Prologue

This book focuses on the ecology of digital racism by mapping the dynamics of three constitutive elements: *Networks – Algorithms – Scale*. These elements organize the book into three key parts. Digital racism is examined through its conditions of emergence, propagation and mutation, via an analysis of (i) networked connectivity as control, (ii) computational algorithmic power, and (iii) the scaling of affective media flows.[1]

Networks are an over-arching structure that organize the digital landscape. They have 'become a defining concept of our epoch' (Chun 2015, 289). Part I of the book identifies how digital networks are governed by a *racial logic* of control (cf. Deleuze 1992; Galloway 2004). Networks appear non-hierarchically structured without a ruling authority, and can be harnessed (and celebrated) for making rhizomatic connections. However, networks are understood as an episteme (Mejias 2013) beyond their alluring visualizations of nodes and links as found in data-network science. It is argued that the networked medium can be exploited, entrenching and distending racialized inequities. Networks spawn the capacious racial logics of hyper-connectivity, differential inclusion and *control* in digital culture.

Algorithms invisibly governing everyday life are examined in Part II. With the expansion of computational power and the production of 'big data', 'machine-learning' algorithms are being utilized to automate decision-making processes and purportedly increase efficiency and accuracy. While the widespread deployment of algorithmic systems or so-called 'Artificial Intelligence' (AI) continues, their 'bias' and potential for perpetuating racial inequalities have been progressively highlighted. However, the grounds on which algorithms are challenged need further scrutiny. I unpack how algorithms address social problems in terms of 'calculative control' (Hong 2022). In particular, the limits of notions of 'bias' are raised by conceiving algorithms as racializing assemblages (Weheliye 2014; Kafer 2019). Their 'black-boxed' lack of transparency is further analysed for obfuscating more complex post-racial processes, to grasp the generative capacities of machine-learning algorithms as *'race-making'* technologies of social control.

Scale offers an approach for analysing how racism is manifested in online spaces and social media platforms. Part III addresses the challenge to grasp the dynamic, multi-modal characteristics of digital racism. I dismiss the catch-all moniker of 'online hate' for displacing a critical understanding of racism, and lacking a sociotechnical approach to analysing online racism. Alternatively, from a perspective of 'scale' (Horton 2021) online racism is conceived as an affective flow of power, concerning its *emergent racial formations*. Scale enables digital racism to be conceived as operating with differing temporalities and dimensions. Furthermore, by characterizing the medium of networked online spaces as a 'complex system' governed by a power law distribution, two key scalings of online racism are identified as *'spectacular'* and *'ambient'* racism. The spectacular risks banalizing racism, while the attritional effects of the ambient are readily overlooked. By scaling racism, it is possible to analyse the differential characteristics and affective flows of online racism as dynamic sociotechnical phenomena.

'DEFINITIONS'

Digital Racism

One of the challenges of studying computational-based, technological forms of racism ('techno-racism') is analysing its divergent characteristics, whether it is the racist outputs of AI chatbots, irreverent viral memes, racially coded micro-aggressions, swarming of users targeting people of colour on social media, algorithmic recommendation running amok or the licentious racial profiling of policing and counter-terrorist surveillance systems. The variance and complexity of techno-racism has unsurprisingly led to an absence of its 'meta-theorization', resulting in piecemeal knowledge which has hindered establishing it as a field of study (cf. Daniels 2013; Kolko et al. 2000).

The multi-modality of techno-racism points to developing interdisciplinary approaches – which is easier said than done. While the study of societal racism has a long history, understanding how it is manifested and *transformed* in digital spaces is an evolving area of research. The important work of scholars such as Ruha Benjamin (2019), Simone Browne (2015) and Safiya Noble (2018) has revealed how digital technologies entrench existing racial inequities, and create new types of exclusions and violence. This work has catalysed critical race and data justice projects, maintaining it is not possible to divorce colonial histories of racial (and other intersectional) oppressions from the development and impact of digital technologies.

My book aims to build on this work by studying contemporary digital technologies as *race-making*. When attempting to conceptualize techno-racism, it is difficult to avoid assuming that it is more or less a continuation or iteration of existing forms of racism that are mediated by technology. This kind of 'social determination of technology' perspective (cf. Winner 1980) begs the question of whether adequate attention has been paid to digital processes and environments through which contemporary techno-racism materializes. Conversely, the trap of technological determinism valorizes the digital medium and fails to address the enduring histories of racial oppression (Nakamura 2013).[2]

As an alternative, I explore the *sociotechnical* production of racism by addressing its entanglements with digital technologies. That is, to unpack the racialization of the digital and the digitalization of the racial.[3] A starting point is to propose that racism is tantamount to a *feature*, and not merely a 'bug' (error or aberration), of digital technologies. The computer industry joke, that a bug can be turned into a feature by simply acknowledging or documenting it (Carr 2018), has profound significance when features enact social harm. For instance, the developers of predictive policing or AI chatbots claiming they cannot fully anticipate the 'downstream societal effects' of their technologies (Moss et al. 2019), effectively deny and obfuscate how racism is 'baked-in' into their systems and the environments these systems operate in.

My focus grapples with the power of the *digital*, 'understood as irreducible, as affecting most if not all areas of social life, and as itself generative of new social practices, ties and relations' (Marres 2017, 14).[4] I want to take seriously the provocation that 'Race itself has become a digital medium' (Nakamura & Chow-White 2012, 5), in relation to the *post-racial transformations* of racism. The post-racial marks the mutability of contemporary racism. The unique features of techno-racism grounded in the medium of the digital, is what I call *Digital Racism*. I present digital racism as an ecology of racializing power – an *emergent* force constituted through the entanglements of the social and the technical. This position echoes the standpoint that digital technologies have 'agency' and are far from neutral. They are imbued with values leading to political consequences (Amoore 2021; McQuillan 2022; Winner 1980).

Moreover, with the hope that 'theory is always a detour on the way to something more important' (Hall 1991, 42), my project is loosely influenced by 'new materialist' approaches to grasp the intersections of race and technology.[5] Put simply, new materialism informs us that 'the social', 'the human', technology or any object is neither a priori or determinate; rather they can be

considered as relational and 'assembled' (Clough 2015). And more specifically, digital materiality can be understood as

> configured by human actors, tools and technologies in an intricate web of mutu-
> ally shaping relations . . . [T]he lines separating objects, actions, and actors
> are hard to draw, as they are hybridized in technological affordances, software
> configurations and user interfaces. (van den Boomen et al. 2009, 10)

My approach to digital materiality is based on two key concepts – *assemblages* and *post-raciality* – as elaborated in the discussion below.

Assemblages

The materiality of digital racism can be explored through the concept of the
'assemblage'. Assemblages are processes through which heterogeneous elements are arranged and connected in particular sets of relations. These relations produce forms of regularity, yet are open to transformation (Deleuze
and Guattari 1987). The 'flat ontology' of assemblages suggests that traditional divisions such as subject/object, material/immaterial, structure/agency
can be rethought (DeLanda 2016). Though, it is worth noting that the term
'assemblages' has become over-wrought, and its 'flat ontology' – similarly
with actor-network-theory – can literally flatten out critical analyses of power
relations.

   My use of assemblage theory seeks to centre power in studying the sociotechnical entanglements of digital racism. Assemblages involve 'affects',
allowing for the recognition of agency beyond only humans. Agency is the
flow of affects in the formation, breakdown and re-formation of assemblages.
It is tied to *power* – the capacity of an object to affect and be affected; not
so much what it is, but what it is capable of *doing* (Massumi 1995). Assemblages enable us to consider race, gender and sexuality as agential flows of
power and resistance.

   Racism conceived as an 'assemblage' is tricky to grasp, because it shifts
conventional ways of thinking about race. It can reveal how the force and
violence of digital race-making emerges through the entanglements of users,
networked connectivity, algorithmic processes, surveillance and platform
economies. This approach does not dwell on regarding race as a spurious
biological invention or a problem of representation. Conventional social sciences and humanities thinking maintains 'race is a social construct' – while
it has no basis in reality, it has real effects in society. But this way of thinking rather inadequately deals with the *materiality* of race. 'Race emerges in
the assemblage, not on its own, but in articulation' (Vila and Avery-Natale
2020, 849). These articulations can take varying forms, and are not limited to
its biological essentialism or social construction. There is nothing essential

about race and nor is it merely a social construct. Race can be considered as multiply articulated and being constantly re/made

> a precarious, open-ended achievement constituted through diverse relations and connections between material and conceptual elements that might include skin colour, segregation, clothing, religion, colonialism, DNA . . . language, migration, and fear. (Swanton 2010, 2238)

Conceived as an assemblage, the focus shifts to how race becomes or emerges via flows of affect, and in particular, how it might aggregate into formations producing racial classifications and effects. The coalescing of affects assemble and systematize objects or 'bodies' into collectivities (Fox and Alldred 2015). Arun Saldanha (2007) offers an account of racializing affects:

> race is not something inscribed upon or referring to bodies, but a particular spatiotemporal disciplining and charging of those bodies themselves. Bodies collectively start behaving like situationally distinct aggregates – racial formations, racial clusters. These clusters emerge immanently, without external blueprint, through the corporeal habits and connections with the environment that bodies necessarily engage in (190).[6]

Digital racism is conceived as an *emergent* phenomenon, manifested when affective flows of race and technology are arrested from becoming otherwise (Sharma 2013). Racism fixes, sorts, differentiates and excludes certain populations. Digital racism arises when computational technologies become *charged* by race; when the affective flows of stereotypes, profiling, othering, anger, fear and whiteness congeal and become attached to, and entangled with, digital technologies (cf. Ahmed 2004). The stickiness or 'viscosity' of race is most apparent in formations of whiteness. Its force normalizes racialized divisions, exclusions and violence. It could be said that AI conversational agents (e.g. OpenAI's ChatGPT) operate via an invisible norm of whiteness, which obfuscates and derogates the downstream discriminatory effects of this technology.

Post-Racial

The protean characteristics and motility of racism have been noted by scholars (Hall 1996; Goldberg 2015; Stoler 1995). Yet, understanding how these are manifested through digital technologies remains challenging. To explore the digital materiality of racism involves being attentive to its *transformations*. Table 1 maps three shifting modalities of racial power. I focus on grasping digital racism through the condition of post-raciality. Needless to

Table 1   Modalities of Racial Power

	Racial Difference	*Power*	*Other*
Colonial Imperialism 'Bounded Space'	Biology *Racism with race – Racial science*	Sovereign-Disciplinary Power *Exclusion*	Immobilized *Negation*
Post-Colonial Globalization 'Networked Space'	Culture *'Racism without race' – Representation*	Biopower *Differential Inclusion*	Breaching borders *Transgression*
Post-Racial Neoliberalism 'Fluid Space'	Computation-Datafication *'Racism without racism' – Emergence*	Biopolitical Security-Control *Modulation – Integration*	Everywhere *Contagion*

say, the mapping is insufficient and should be read as a schema attempting to capture the motility of racism, its entanglements and dis/continuities.[7]

The post-racial is a slippery and somewhat redundant term. Nonetheless, the post-racial can be mined for revealing contemporary transformations of racism. As with all 'posts-' the problem of periodization is not easy to resolve, and I want to avoid presenting the post-racial as superseding earlier racial forms. Sarah Banet-Weiser et al. (2019) reflect on this concern and state: 'We approach postrace as the racial project of our time' (5). Similarly, David Theo Goldberg (2015) intimates the paradoxical condition of the post-racial because it 'is the most racial'. These authors insist that the post-racial does not herald the waning of the effects of racism, as celebrated with the 2008 U.S. presidential election of Barack Obama. Not only are new modes of techno-racism emerging, colonial and post-colonial forms of racial power endure in neoliberal, post-racial conditions. Everyday exclusions and impoverishment, the resurgence of white nationalism, the killings of people of colour, their mass incarceration and disproportionate impact of COVID-19 are all symptomatic of the necropolitical violence of past and present forms of racism (Mbembe 2003; Sandset 2021; Sexton 2015).

Neoliberalism's usurping of the social fabric of society has profoundly affected manifestations of contemporary race and racism. Goldberg (2015) dissects the operations of post-racial neoliberalism in his discussion of the privatization of the social.

In keeping with the neoliberalizing thrusts of individualization, self-making, and the proliferation of enterprise, the postracial condition doubles racial response. Responsibility for racist expression is reduced to an individualized account, to a bad apple, a rogue element. This denies responsibility to structural conditions or larger social forces. For neoliberalizing postraciality, racism is an anomaly, the mark of a past historical moment (64).

In comparison, for post-colonial forms of racism, 'culture' and 'difference' encode or operate as proxies of race (Gilroy 1987). And as Eduardo Bonilla-Silva (2006) has argued, racism can function 'without racists' in assertions of colour-blindness that uphold white supremacy. Goldberg (2015) extends this account by stressing how the post-racial condition is making referents of race inchoate and impervious to interrogate, thereby disrupting our capacity to assay insurgent forms of racism:

> neoliberal postraciality amounts to 'racisms without racism' . . . This is the enigmatic condition of the circulation of racisms, renewed, reinvented, resurrected, born again though never dead, without the terms to name it as such, to identify, comprehend, or condemn (81–82).

The post-racial marks an intensive *mutability* of racism that refutes its own systemic, enduring presence. Mainstream accounts of race are discursively framed by the pretension that racism no longer matters – reduced to anomalous or socially aberrant outbreaks. The post-racial condition confounds, obfuscates and disavows the salience and pervasiveness of racism. The 'post' in post-race is 'the critical affirmation of proliferations of racism in a contemporary neoliberal order that claims to have gone beyond the racial' (Sharma & Sharma 2012).

Table 1 indicates colonial racism founded on lineage/biological difference, and post-colonial racism is also determined by cultural differences. With regard to post-raciality, additionally, it is a racism predicated on the computational processing of data, or more precisely, *datafication*. Datafication refers to processes that abstract almost any aspect of our lives into measures and classification, for the purpose of extraction, optimization and greater control (Mejias and Couldry 2019; D'Ignazio and Klein 2020).

The post-racial can situate the transformations and mutations of contemporary racism in relation to burgeoning digital technologies. A globalizing culture foments mobilities, hyper-connectivity and networked contagions, which breach boundaries and irrupt 'real' and 'virtual' borders. The racism of modernity sought to fix discrepant bodies as objects of disciplinary knowledge and containment. In contrast, the post-racial provokes the *emergent* – a mode of interventionary race-making – in an era of in/security. The condition of post-raciality reveals how racism is permuted via the tension between containment and the biopolitical management of the threat of an itinerant otherness.

> The racial needs no determinism (sociocultural or biological) to function in this case. And racism cannot enclose, contain and purify spaces to the same extent and on the same scale as it once did. Not a racism of hegemony or antagonisms, but one of perpetual contestation. (Valayden 2013, 137)[8]

A digital racism of 'perpetual contestation' gives rise to its mutability and proliferation, while simultaneously obfuscating post-racial regimes of control.

HOW TO READ THIS BOOK

I explore the complexity and multi-modality of digital racism by developing an interdisciplinary approach that is not limited to a particular paradigm or theory. My project is rather exploratory and experimental in terms of working outside of disciplinary boundaries to address the *intersections* of race, technology and power. There is a risk with interdisciplinary work that it does not cohere or lacks depth. This book contributes to ongoing debates, and offers a series of discussion points and contentions to open up novel lines of inquiry. It may challenge readers to consider alternative approaches to studying technological forms of racism.

While the book is organized thematically into three main parts, each can be read independently. The analysis does not provide exhaustive or definitive answers to the problem of digital racism. Not only is digital racism complex and multifaceted, but it is also constantly evolving and shifting. I offer an approach that focuses on fundamental sociotechnical elements of *Networks*, *Algorithms* and *Scale* that I believe will remain relevant.

The main purpose of this book is to understand the complexity of contemporary digital racism. It becomes apparent that there are no straightforward solutions to overcome the seeming inexorability of digital racism. This does not suggest digital racism is insurmountable. To imply that it is not possible to overcome racism, technological or otherwise, belies the long and enduring histories of anti-racist struggle and resistance to domination. We need to keep striving for ways to confront digital racism.

In the *Epilogue*, I seek out how digital racism may be resisted. What is presented is by no means conclusive. My intention is more *speculative*, inspired by abolitionist and Afrofuturist thinking that re-imagine alternatives technological futures, beyond the interests of Big Tech and governmental control. I raise a number of propositions and provocations that explore possibilities of overcoming digital racism. The aim is to equip readers to challenge, obviate and eradicate digital racism.

NOTES

1. Identifying 'Networks', 'Algorithms' and 'Scale' offers particular ways to open up an analysis of digital racism. These are considered to be fundamental to addressing

the complexity of how race, technology and power intersect. Without a doubt, there are many other possible approaches.

2. Part III examines the limits of both social and technological determinism regarding how to grasp contemporary forms of digital racism. My approach is informed by a 'digital methods' perspective, which proposes to 'follow the medium' (Rogers 2013) while appreciating the social formation of digital spaces.

3. I'm thankful to Jas Nijjar for prompting me to consider this formulation.

4. To expound the ontological status and meaning of the 'digital' is beyond the scope of my short book. The digital can be understood as a process of abstraction, rendering the world into code that can be computationally processed at scale. With advances in neoliberal technological innovation and computing power, it has led to increasing the capacities of datafication and control. For notable accounts of the digital, see Chun (2011) and Hui (2016).

5. 'New Materialism' covers a divergent body of work, exploring the capacities, entanglements and emergent agencies of 'humans' and 'non-humans'. I am aware of its limits concerning analysing relations of power and engaging with feminist, queer and critical race theories. For a useful discussion, see Chad Shomura (2017).

6. The Deleuzo-Guattarian figure of the 'body' is and active agent in a state of constant transformation. It can refer to human and non-human, animate and inanimate objects.

7. Figure 1 is discussed in greater depth in Part I. Developing this schema has been influenced by a range of thinkers, including Benjamin (2019), Deleuze and Guattari (1987), Goldberg (2015), Mol and Law (1994) and Saldanha (2007).

8. I would like to thank David T. Goldberg for drawing my attention to the doctoral work of Valayden (2013).

Part I

Networks

The film *Snowden* (2016) dramatizes the life of the ex-CIA analyst. Edward Snowden sensationally leaked highly classified information concerning the U.S. National Security Agency (NSA) clandestine digital operations across the globe. There is a stand-out scene in the film which visualizes a 'network', revealing chilling NSA anti-terrorist online surveillance practices. We see how a 'person of interest' is targeted by mapping their immediate connections with family members, friends and contacts; in turn, these secondary figures spawn further links to others . . . and so the network expands. It leads to the ensnaring of potentially millions of loosely connected individuals, merely linked *by association* as possible suspects. This is the paranoid network logic of mass surveillance (cf. Hu 2015).

The event of 11 September 2001 (9/11) attacks against the United States ushered in the egregious Patriot Act and online surveillance at scale. Mohammed Atta was identified as a pivotal figure responsible for 9/11. Arguably, it was the *method* of determining Atta as a principal instigator of the attacks that led to the NSA embracing 'network science' in their digital efforts to identify invisible terrorists hidden among the general population.

One year after 9/11, the network analyst Valdis Krebs (2002) published an innovatory article entitled 'Uncloaking Terrorist Networks'. Krebs used publicly available communications (meta-)data to map the network of the nineteen dead hijackers. Networks are essentially composed of connections or 'links' (relationships and interactions) of discrete elements or 'nodes' (such as individuals, groups or organizations). Krebs's resourceful application of network theory identified Atta as a crucial node, a 'broker' linking or bridging other ostensibly unconnected individuals. Based on the analysis by Krebs, the 9/11 network could have been dismantled if merely three of its central nodes had been 'eliminated' (Keefe 2006).

1

The 'new' science of networks is exalted for revealing multifarious, hidden patterns and associations, which otherwise appear impossible to see or grasp. Networks are everywhere. Or rather, the network imagination is everywhere. It is found in modelling biological processes, city planning, climate change, our social relations and the internet itself. Network analyses fundamentally explore *connectivity*, aiming to capture and visualize the messy contingent realities of the world. Networks are frameworks operating as social technologies, as well as technical infrastructures (Chun 2019). Wendy Hui Kyong Chun reminds us that network modelling is a 'dramatic simplifications of real world phenomena . . . with each phase of network theory – initial abstraction/representation followed by mathematical modeling – producing its own type of abstraction' (70). While the mathematical study of networks (graph theory) is not new; the rise of network science and its fetishized data modelling and visualizations over the last two decades has surged across the natural and social sciences.

Geert Lovink (2012) urges us to critically think of networks beyond traditional organizational structures: 'the social manifests itself as a network. Networked practices emerge outside the walls of twentieth-century institutions, leading to a "corrosion of conformity". The network is the actual shape of the social' (3). To that end, Ulises Ali Mejias (2013) is cognisant of the pitfalls in reifying digital networks. Yet considers it 'necessary to isolate the network as a single epistemic form' to enable identifying the 'common forms of violence found across all forms of networked participation' (xiii).

I explore how insurgent modes of *racism* are entangled and propagated by networks. To unpack the claim that racism is *networked,* my discussion is organized into three sections, examining networks via infrastructural inequalities, modes of control and abject social connectivity. Section one sets things up to highlight the skewed topology of networks in relation to prevailing neoliberal logics. The next section develops an account of *post-racial control,* by bringing into dialogue influential accounts of 'networks and control' (Deleuze 1992; Galloway 2004), with 'bio-power and post-raciality' (Foucault 2004; Goldberg 2015). Networks, neoliberalism and post-racial dynamics are interconnected. As networks adhere to neoliberal logics, their politics operate through a post-racial framework, a crucial facet of neoliberalism. And to ground the discussion, the third section delves into the lasting impact of the 'Alt-Right' in propagating networked racism. Online crowds and contagion are explored to account for how digital racism proliferates while rendered intractable in an age of networks.

NETWORKED DISCREPANCY

The internet, commonly described as the 'network of networks', is often represented as formed by *horizontal* connections that are adaptable, in comparison to traditional, ossified vertical or centralized modes of organization. The internet has the inordinate capacity to expand its connections. As a data communications transmission network, its 1960s Cold War military-academic origins innovated a *decentralized* design (Baran 1964). Rather than a single point of failure of centralized systems, a distributed topology was considered more resilient to maintain 'command and control' in the aftermath of a nuclear assault.

The evolution of a publicly accessible internet – underpinned by private–corporate interests and infrastructure – has been possible because of its open architecture (Terranova 2004). It's a technological triumph that any device, whether a computer, smartphone or sensor, with the requiste protocols can connect to any other device on the internet. Digital connectivity spurred a democratizing shift from centralized one-to-many to peer 'many-to-many' modes of communication, interaction and participation. There is no blue-print or master-plan for the internet – it appears to lack a controlling authority because of its decentralized design. Horizontal flows of data dynamically re-route through the network because of the ingenuity of 'packet-switching' via the TCP/IP (Transmission Control Protocol/Internet Protocol) developed in the 1980s (Galloway 2004).

When the computer scientist and activist, John Gilmore claimed 'The Net interprets censorship as damage and routes around it' (cited in Rheingold 2000, 8), he was celebrating the internet's techno-political capacity of freedom of communication. This kind of vision was famously articulated in the manifesto, *A Declaration of the Independence of Cyberspace* by John Barlow (1996), which proclaimed the internet as a space of autonomy and agency. Alongside Gilmore, Barlow was a co-founder of the Electronic Frontier Foundation (EFF), a non-profit organization set up to defend civil liberties, user privacy and free expression for the digital world. In his manifesto, Barlow polemically wrote:

> Governments of the Industrial World, you weary giants of flesh and steel, I come from Cyberspace, the new home of Mind. On behalf of the future, I ask you of the past to leave us alone. You are not welcome among us. You have no sovereignty where we gather. [. . .] We are creating a world that all may enter without privilege or prejudice accorded by race, economic power, military force, or station of birth (Barlow 1996).

There has been much debate whether Barlow – also a lyricist for the *Grateful Dead!* – was a naive techno-utopian, or imagined 'another world is possible' in which the internet will emancipate rather than oppress (Doctorow 2019). He believed that inclusion and participation in the network were essential for maintaining freedom.

In hindsight, '[i]nequality is, in fact, part of the natural order of networks' (Mejias 2013, 4). Networks can be skewed in their topology – the arrangement of links are not random or evenly distributed. The work of Albert-László Barabási (2009) demonstrated that the internet basically follows a logarithmic or power law distribution: relatively few numbers of nodes (hubs) have the majority of links; while the many remaining nodes have relatively few connections.[1] It results in key hubs potentially wielding considerable impact in a network, as data emanates or passes through these super-connectors. These kinds of networks can exhibit a 'small-world' phenomenon, which effectively reduces 'distances' across a network.

A principal property of these 'scale-free' networks is that they retain their underlying strucutre as they grow. Thus, the inequality of unevenly distributed links is compounded by how scale-free networks expand (Barabási 2009). Rather than all nodes having an equal chance to attract new links, existing central hubs are more likely to be connected by new nodes joining the network. This phenomenon of 'preferential attachment' or the 'rich get richer' principle, is strikingly visible on popular social media platforms such as Twitter and Instagram. Celebrities and other public figures can amass millions of followers, while the majority of ordinary users struggle to acquire significant numbers. Moreover, as Mejias (2013) points out, rich nodes getting richer

> is not something that should strike us as illogical or irrational, since we know that even (or especially) in the midst of great disparity, those with resources manage to increase their wealth at the expense of those with few resources (4).

Barlow's cyberlibertarian manifesto paid little attention to discrepant network architectures and rebutted the intrusion of nation-state governments, in order for the internet to exist without borders or authority. In contrast, Alexander Galloway (2004) spurns the idea of the internet as some kind of autonomous or self-determining space:

> the founding principle of the Net is control, not freedom – control has existed from the beginning. Perhaps it is a different type of control than we are used to seeing. It is a type of control based on openness, inclusion, universalism, and flexibility (142).

The internet, as a distributed system, gives the impression of freedom because information is designed to flow as freely as possible. In comparison, decentralized systems limit paths of information flow, and in centralized systems, the paths are predetermined. Galloway maintains that while there are no centralized points of control in a distributed system, 'protocol is how technological control exists after decentralization' (2004, 8). That is, control is nonetheless operational via protological 'rules' and 'regulations' of interoperability and standardization. Protological control dynamically operates in distributed digital spaces as a technology of connection, inclusion and integration.

If Barlow failed to consider how networks can (re)produce inequalities, he also did not foresee the subsequent technocultural dominance of a neoliberal 'Californian ideology' (Barbrook and Cameron 1996). In the Global North, the hegemony of a handful of Silicon Valley technology-based corporate giants – *not* governments – have inordinately shaped the internet. The 'Big Five' or 'Big Tech' transnational companies – Google/Alphabet, Apple Facebook/Meta, Amazon and Microsoft (GAFAM) – dominate the digital landscape (Kwet 2019).[2] By exploiting the discrepant characteristics of networks, these corporations gained significant control over how we communicate and participate on the internet. It is the *lack* of governmental regulation, antitrust enforcement and unfettered neoliberal marketization that has led to an internet far from what Barlow envisioned (Doctorow, 2019). There is no irony in the opening statement of the book, *The New Digital Age* co-authored by Eric Schmidt (former Google CEO) when it is declared: 'the online world is not truly bound by terrestrial laws . . . it's the world's largest ungoverned space' (Schmidt et al. 2014, 3).

Big Tech has arrogated the open architecture of the internet and asserted its restricted communication networks. Until the late 1990s, the majority of public communications over the internet took place via *open* protocols, such as HTTP (web), SMPT (email) and Internet Relay Chat (IRC). Today, most online communications are determined by closed, propriety services (van Dijck 2013), increasingly in the form of popular social media platforms and smartphone apps such Facebook Messenger and WhatsApp (also owned by Meta). Recall that the internet is the *infrastructure* for online communications, and the web, for example, is a particular set of protocols for utilizing the internet. By harnessing interactive Web 2.0 technologies, Big Tech developed bounded digital platforms and apps, which afford online interactions as convenient, creative and 'addictive', leading to vast numbers of users – unwittingly or resigned to – being entrapped in the 'walled gardens' of social media (Seymour 2019). In the hands of Big Tech, digital networks operate with logics of hyper-connectivity, ubiquitous data capture and inescapable user participation, which are consonant with neoliberal market rationalities of late capitalism (Couldry and Mejias 2019; Srnicek 2016).

Digital networks are not immanently neoliberal, nonetheless, as Chun (2015) maintains, 'networks have been central to the emergence, management and imaginary of neoliberalism, in particular to its narrative of individuals collectively dissolving society' (289). Over the last few decades, neoliberalism has assailed social welfare and collective representation, deepened poverty and exacerbated social decracination and racial inequalities.

Neoliberalism has promoted politico-economic rationalities of privatization, de-regulation and risk management, chronic financial instability, enterprise and possessive individualism, and the unbridled datafication of society (Brown 2017; Van Dijck 2013).

The adage *'You are the Product'* embodies the neoliberal business practices of providing 'free' online communication services to billions of people across the globe. Beyond the rise of a public 'techlash' discourse (Atkinson et al. 2019), critical internet studies scholars have been discussing the unwieldly power of Big Tech and their obfuscated practices of monetizing user data (Andrejevic et al. 2015). But only recently did it come to light the astonishing depths of data-mining operations and rampant sharing of user information with unregulated data-brokers.

The scandalous case of the political 'consulting firm,' Cambridge Analytica and Facebook laid bare the fallacy of data privacy claims of corporate social media platforms whose business models are built and utterly dependent upon surveillance capitalism (Zuboff 2019). Without the knowledge or consent of millions of Facebook users, their raw profile data was exposed to Cambridge Analytica. The firm's vice president was the odious white nationalist Steve Bannon, and the information garnered from Facebook users was illicitly deployed to promote the 2016 Donald Trump election campaign.

Shoshana Zuboff's (2019) account of *surveillance capitalism* reveals how data-mining and user-tracking technologies have revolutionized the commodification of online human experience. Zuboff identifies a 'behavioural surplus' – data trails and everyday online activities generated by users – as the new logic of capitalist 'accumulation by dispossession'[3] of Big Tech. She discusses how maps of North America labelled whole areas of native peoples as 'heathens' and 'primitives', erasing their humanity and legitimating acts of dispossession and expropriation. Zuboff draws a (problematic) comparison by contending we, as contemporary digital users, are the 'natives' in relation to how: 'claims to self-determination have vanished from the maps of our own behavior. They are erased in an astonishing and audacious act of dispossession by surveillance' (2016). Companies such as Facebook and Google depend on the ceaseless process of the 'digital dispossession' of online behaviour. Behavioural surplus is used to micro-target and predict our future actions. It is transformed into a propriety product essential to the workings of digital corporations, and traded in the recondite multi-million dollar data analytics market-place.

Unlike Zuboff who egregiously uses colonialism as a metaphor, Nick Couldry and Ulises Mejias (2019) claim we are encountering a new *techno-colonial reality* in their trenchant analysis of digital media corporations.[4] They contend that *data colonialism* involves 'the extraction of value through data represents a new form of resource appropriation on a par with the land-grab (the seizure of land, resources and labour) that kicked off historical colonialism' (3). Data colonialism constitutes digital connectivity as inevitable, and networked user participation as compulsory. A new order is emerging, and the datafication of the *social* is a crucial step in the new capitalist phase of data colonialism. The social is being transposed into datafied relations which expropriate value from our online activities. 'Digital platforms are the technological means that produce a new type of "social" for capital: that is, the social in a form that can be continuously tracked, captured, sorted, and counted for value as "data"' (Couldry and Mejias 2018, 6).

The telling critiques of surveillance capitalism and data colonialism expose the veracity of neoliberal market logics of digital media that are subsuming everyday life. Although, the deployment of the term 'colonialism' in the analysis has unsurprisingly come under scrutiny. María Soledad Segura and Silvio Waisbord (2019) stress 'colonialism is unthinkable without violence – the takeover of lands and populations by sheer physical force' (416). The work of Couldry and Mejias (2019) is cognizant of the histories of colonialism, and their intervention in developing a critical digital media studies is far-reaching. Nonetheless, conjoining the terms 'data' and 'colonialism' for studying digital dispossession and expropriation requires careful consideration in terms of existing unevenly distributed technologies, *racial* power and control, historical periodization, differing regimes of settler colonialism and unequal geographies across the world.

Despite the acceleration of transnational state-corporate technology collusions across North-South divide, conceptually connecting data with colonialism can inadvertently universalize discourses from the Global North (Mumford 2022; Segura and Waisbord 2019). The analysis is further complicated by forms of racialized data mining operating in the Global South. For example, identification and biometric profiling such as finger-printing was first tested on colonized populations during the nineteenth century (Heynen and van der Muelen 2019; Sengoopta 2003). More recently, surveillant ID cards have been trialled in refugee camps, and development aid in war-torn regions is tied to state-corporate forms of biopolitical population management (Dongus 2019).

The data colonialism focus on capitalist resource extraction tends to underplay the originary force of *coloniality* in the epistemic centring of European domination (Mumford 2022). It omits a sustained analysis of *race and racism* – as part of a wider 'colonial matrix of power' (Quijano and Ennis 2000) – which has been integral to coloniality and its surveillant practices (Browne 2015). This omission leads to a lack of focus on the divergent and shifting modalities of *race* as a technology of power (Gray 2019; Franklin 2018; Puar 2017). It is this concern that I turn to next, specifically in relation to developing an account of *post-raciality*, control and digital networks in Western societies.[5]

POST-RACIAL CONTROL

The *Prologue* presents a schema loosely mapping the colonial, post-colonial and post-racial onto sovereign, disciplinary and control (governmentality-security) technologies of power, respectively (see table 1). 'Control names a dynamic mode of power which seeks to proliferate difference in order to modulate and contain its disruptive force' (Ahuja 2018, 47). However, mapping these shifts of power is not straightforward. Herman S. Gray (2019) troubles any singular or linear periodizing of the post-racial by suggesting the notion of 'spacetime,' which considers the inchoate and discordant ways that race is operating today.

> Thinking the postracial in terms of the spacetime of race lines up with the shift in the nature of power knowledge that produces race and on which its practices depend and the nature of the society – in this case society of control – in which it operates (26).

Gray explores, alongside a handful of authors – see especially Neel Ahuja (2018) and Jasbir Puar (2017) – how *race* intersects with *control* and net-worked power, which has been largely bereft in influential new materialist studies of technology such as Deleuze (1992), Galloway (2004) and Hardt and Negri (2000).

Deleuze's essay, *Post-script to the Societies of Control* was strikingly suc-cinct, yet remains formative in claiming we are in the midst of new type of distributed power based on computer technologies. In mapping this shift of power in Western nations, he draws upon Foucault (1997, 2007). Briefly put, *sovereign* power (centralized/hierarchical) is characterized as law-like and violent, coercive and prohibitive, visibly emanating from a figure of author-ity. In contrast, *disciplinary* power (decentralized/bureaucratic) emerging during the rise of capitalism in the eighteenth and nineteenth centuries is less visible and operates in spaces of enclosure such as the prisons, factories, schools and families. The individual is moulded or 'trained' by these insti-tutions. This kind of 'productive' power shapes and normalizes individuals into docile bodies. According to Deleuze, these institutions came into crisis (especially after World War II), and the task of disciplining individuals as they move through institutions has become increasingly diffused.

A shift to *societies of control* (distributed/protological) engenders dis-persed architectures of power that do not directly manage populations through enclosures. Deleuze (1992) writes: 'Enclosures are molds, distinct castings, but controls are a modulation, like a self-deforming cast that will continuously change from one moment to the other' (4). In an interview, he invokes the 'highway' to illustrate the workings of control: 'You do not confine people with a highway. But by making highways, you multiply the means of control . . . people can travel infinitely and "freely" without being confined while being perfectly controlled. This is our future' (Deleuze 2006, 322). While the concept of control remains prescient as a digital technology of power, its analysis of inequalities and exclusions are decidedly sketchy. Nonetheless, reading Deleuze *via Foucault* can help develop an understanding of how *race* and *racism* intersect with control.

Foucault's geneaological approach avoids universalizing racism – it is not a natural or inevitable phenomenon. He maintains that transitions in forms of societal power are not merely a series of successions (Foucault 2007). The distinctions are to do with the changing modes of social control. In particular, he identifies two forms or 'poles' of biopower emerging during the eighteenth century: an anatomo-politics of the body; and, subsequently, a biopolitics of the population. The former is linked with disciplinary practices of prisons and schools, for example; and the latter with pervasive governmental controls. In contrast to the binaristic discontinuity of life and death of sovereign power, biopolitics operates as a continuous and regulatory mechanism targeting the *life of the population*. Sovereign-juridical power is about law and coercion, wielded when there are infractions. Biopolitics is concerned with conformity and *norms*, functioning without interruption (Puar 2017). Crucially, biopolitics is entangled with and activated by racism. Racism *underpins* the biopolitical emergence of 'security' in nineteenth-century Europe – the need to protect the population against (internal) threats from contagion, the other, the abnormal (Macey 2009; McWhorter 2009).[6]

The relationship between biopower and modern racism is predicated on notions of the 'normal' and 'abnormal', which is useful to explore further. In *Abnormal: Lectures at the Collège de France 1974-1975*, Foucault (2003) identifies a 'racism against the abnormal'. The norm, in disciplinary societies, functions to correct and transform individuals in their domains (enclosures) to a pre-existing standard. An alternative normalizing practice develops in the transition to biopolitical security. Rather than a strong distinction, there is a 'gradation from the normal to the abnormal' (2003, 42). The biopolitical functions through mechanisms of *integration*. Integration seeks to regulate, modulating divisions and differences in a population. For biopolitical power, identifying the normal and abnormal comes before identifying the norm. As Foucault writes: 'We have a plotting of the normal and the abnormal, of different curves of normality . . . The norm is an interplay of differential normalities. The normal comes first and the norm is deduced from it' (2007, 63). Through constant surveillance, measurement and comparison by the security apparatus, collections of 'differential normalities' are generated to perform as the optimal or ideal normal (Taylor 2011). The biopolitical regulates 'degrees of normality' across entire populations (Amoore 2009).

The *post-racial condition* can be grasped via a biopolitics, through which racism functions as a mutable and motile technology of biopower.[7] It generates complex modes of inclusion/exclusion and integration, as observed by Jasbir Puar (2017):

> biopolitical control operates most perniciously and efficiently through reifying intersectional identity frames . . . as the most pertinent ones for political intervention, thus obfuscating forms of control that insidiously include in order to exclude, and exclude in order to include (23).

It is worth reiterating that *disciplinary* (inclusionary/exclusionary) and *biopolitical* (regulatory-integrating) mechanisms are co-articulated as biopower (Foucault 2004). While Deleuze singles out integration and modulation as mechanisms of control, Seb Franklin (2018) offers a more nuanced account highlighting the 'sorting' and 'disposal' functions of biopower: 'biopower operates through and produces thresholds that render legible certain populations while occluding (or rendering as non-populations) certain others' (49). Franklin's account teases out the workings of biopower – how distributed forms of control render 'non-selected' beings as 'structurally invisible', which nonetheless can remain entangled with disciplinary and sovereign forms of racial violence.[8]

The *post-racial* significance of biopower hinges on the intensification of the racially coded production (and obfuscation) of the 'ideal norm': 'the race that holds power and is entitled to define the norm, and against those who deviate from that norm, against those who pose a threat' (Foucault 2004, 61). Thus, in Western societies of security control, contemporary racism serves as a strategy for *defending* an imagined white population. The threat of race, is a threat against white civilization. As Ladelle McWhorter (2009) insists, 'Modern racism is not really about nonwhites; modern racism is really all about white people' (35).

A centring of *whiteness* in accounts of biopolitical racism is evident in how Foucault influenced Deleuze and Guattari (1987). They assert that racism operates by the 'degrees of deviance' from a 'White-Man Face' (norm), which sometimes can tolerate 'nonconforming traits' or at other times erase them. 'The dividing line is not between inside and outside but rather is internal . . . Racism . . . propagates waves of sameness until those who resist identification have been wiped out' (178).

The deviation from a 'white norm' is fundamental to grasping contemporary operations of biopolitical racism. Echoing Deleuze and Guattari, Hardt and Negri (2000) attest that modern racism functions as a strategy of 'differential inclusion', in contrast to the abjection of the Other (Sharma and Sharma 2003). In their sweeping account of *Empire*, they discuss 'real subsumption' having 'no outside' in the expansion of capitalism and mobility. Empire promulgates a neo-racism of integration (differences are ordered and controlled), which is distinguished from colonial racism of boundary maintenance in the European division of Self/Other (differences are excluded and negated).

> White supremacy functions . . . through engaging alterity and then subordinating differences according to degrees of deviance from whiteness . . . Subordination is enacted in regimes of everyday practices that are more mobile and flexible but that create racial hierarchies that are nonetheless stable and brutal. (Hardt and Negri 2000, 194)

Hardt and Negri understand the force of racism as a drive towards integration. Neoliberal *networked* power integrates as it grows, fomenting hyperconnectivity, irrupting borders and unleashing mobilities and contagions of difference. This is congruent with the expansionist drive of communicative capitalism, technically aligned with the open architecture of digital networks designed to continually forge connections with divergent systems (Dean 2010; Terranova 2004). Hardt and Negri bring a semblance of race into the discussion of control and networks. Although their account of networks – as with the notion of *Empire* itself – is rather vague. Mejias (2013), on the other hand, is more exacting. He offers a cogent sociotechnical account of digital networks (though he lacks exploring an analysis of biopolitics and networked racism).

The concept of the 'network episteme' is critical to Mejias's project, because networks have become 'a technological template for organizing the social [and] a knowledge structure, a way of seeing the world as composed of nodes and links' (10). He is troubled that *participation* in networks is effectively obligatory in digital societies. In fact, networks – especially social media platforms and apps – impel participation as they become ubiquitous in determining how we access the internet. To participate online enables social connectivity and digital citizenry. However, the logic of the network episteme produces inequalities through inclusion and exclusion, which Mejias identifies as the politics of nodocentrism:

> the belief that participation in networks creates equality and diversity is, in fact, a rejection of difference, because ways of belonging that do not conform to nodocentrism become an impossibility within the network . . . It privileges nodes while discriminating against what is not a node – the invisible, the Other (27–8).

In comparison to Hardt and Negri avowing there being nothing *outside* of *Empire*, Mejias is more circumspect in elaborating the relationship between networks, control and otherness. He observes that boundaries – vis-à-vis modes of inclusion and exclusion – are the permeable limits of what is between nodes and beyond networks: 'the inequality that digital networks generate revolves around inclusion (inequality among nodes within the network), and exclusion (inequality between nodes and the outsides of networks)'(76). By grappling with the structural invisibility generated by nodocentrism, Mejias can help us to identify how modes of *networked racism* intersect with a normalizing biopolitics.

ALT-RIGHT

To elaborate a discussion of *post-racial* networked racism, I turn to exploring the online phenomenon of the so-called 'Alt-Right', because of its strong association with nefariously utilizing digital communications.[9] Silicon Valley's neoliberal ideology does not see racism (or any other inequality) as formative to the exploitation of networked communications (Benjamin 2019; Daniels 2018; Noble 2018). Inundatory social connectivity and information flows of digital networks have been manipulated by the Alt-Right. Notwithstanding the entanglement of the Alt-Right with 'Alt-Tech' – right-leaning software developers and entrepreneurs in the tech industry (Fielitz et al. 2019) – it is misguided to think that the Alt-Right only hijack and mis-use digital networks to propagate their offensive ideas and harassment campaigns. We must acknowledge how pervasive technologies of the networked environment have been *integral* to the Alt-Right's impact. 'The rise of the alt-right would not be possible without the infrastructure built by the tech industry, and yet, the industry likes to imagine itself as creating a "race-less" Internet' (Daniels 2018, 62).

Following the defeat of U.S. president Donald Trump in 2020 and the tumultuous attack on the Capitol Building in January 2021 by his 'supporters', the online visibility of the Alt-Right has waned and splintered towards more isolated social media platforms. There was an effort by Big Tech platforms to ban accounts associated with far-right actors. However, Trump's presidency and the Alt-Right 'have acted as a vector to mainstream far-right politics in the US, through the constant shifting between illiberal and liberal articulations of racism and the blurring of boundaries between both' (Mondon and Vaughan 2020). The legacy of the Alt-Right concerning the online *mainstreaming* of racism makes it a compelling case to study its networked techno-politics.

The Alt-Right promoted itself as a radical alternative to traditional conservatism (Angwin 2016). Yet neither was it a coherent movement, nor did it advance a congruous ideology. Its antecedents and influences are connected with white supremacy and ethno-nationalism. The media characterization of the Alt-Right as rebooted fascism neglects understanding its *post-racial* politics. Furthermore, the presentation of the Alt/far right as 'extremist' for- mations can lead to conceiving racism only as a socially aberrant and *excep- tional* phenomena. It belies the normalization of racism and its systemic and everyday (re)production (Daniels 2009; Mondon and Winter 2017).[10]

The Alt-Right has been described as a 'leaderless', anti-globalist far-right reactionary force, vehemently defending white male identity and 'western civilisation', which is believed to be under attack by rampant immigra- tion, social justice warriors (feminists, anti-racists and LGBQT+ rights activists), Islam, black criminality and undermined by liberal democracies enslaved by multicultural diversity, 'wokeness,' political correctness and cancel culture (Hawley 2017; Nagle 2017). The composition of the Alt-Right involves loosely *networked* coalitions, including ultranationalists, mano- sphere misogynists, antagonistic online 'trolling' cultures, and influenced by groups with varying ideological leanings, such as The European New Right, Neo-Reactionaries/Accelerationists and Neo-Fascists/Nazis. Mike Wendling (2018) captures the essence of the Alt-Right: 'an oppositional force with no real organizational structure. It's a creature of the internet . . . It's a movement with several factions which shrink or swell according to the political breeze and the task at hand' (5).

Biopolitics and Fear

Central to emergence of the Alt-Right has been its reaction to biopoliti- cal neoliberalism. Neoliberal policies have enervated social infrastructure, splintered communities and breached borders to accelerate the movement of capital and labour. Neoliberalism potentially puts everyone at risk, as abstract and impersonal 'market forces' determine the politics of life and death of the population – what Henry Giroux (2007) calls the 'biopolitics of disposability'.

Common to the many strands of the Alt-Right is a post-racial identitarian politics of victimhood and ressentiment, not just from the disenfranchised working and lower class, 'but *dethroned whites*, especially white men who have lost not just economic but also social power and cultural pride' (Brown 2017). Neoliberal crisis is reformulated as an apocryphal crisis of white pre- carity. The fear of changing demographics, fuelled by neoliberal globaliza- tion, mass migration, Black Lives Matter demands have spawned ominous conspiracy theories of the 'Great Replacement' and 'White Genocide' that imagine a future of ethnically white populations reduced to a 'minority' status or even extinction (Bhatt 2021). 'Red pilling', to see reality and discover 'the truth' – a popular reference from *The Matrix* (1999) film – is the Alt-Right's liberatory wake-up call (Munn 2019). The toxic beliefs of the collapse of white culture and Western civilization have been linked to horrific acts of extreme-right violence (Davey and Ebner 2019; Bhatt 2021).

The Alt-Right react to the de-stabilizing effects of neoliberalism by 'displacing struggles over control over one's life to struggles against a threatening other' (Macey 2009, 2013). Rather than market rationalities of contemporary capitalism optimizing life of the population, the Alt-Right desire to *re-politicize* the distribution of risk and disposability by biopolitically re-centring whiteness and buttressing white identity. Reasserting white normativity is what appears to confederate the disparate groupings of the Alt-Right. And while racialized minorities manifestly bear the devastation of neoliberal crises, they are mendaciously cast as unworthy, alien and disposable . . . *black lives don't matter*. The Alt-Right's 'aim is to secure the very curves that derive "normality" from the demographics of the majority and to dispossess targeted populations' (Gambetti 2018, 3).

A defining feature of the post-racial condition is that the other is unveiled as dangerously *everywhere*: 'There are only overlaps and intersections, barbarians circulating outside and inside the gates, walls, and boundaries, blurring the very lines themselves' (Goldberg 2015, 121). Not only has this mitigated an Alt-Right backlash of paranoid fear, hostility and offence. It also shapes the modality of what Chandiren Valyden (2013) calls 'outbreak racism'. This is a post-racial racism of 'perpetual contestation', rather than of hegemony and protection of social structures. Lovink echoes Valyden's account more broadly when he says: 'The social, which used to be the glue for repairing historical damage, can quickly turn into unstable, explosive material' (Lovink 2012, 5). The extant racisms of securing the nation waver in their ability to enclose and purify spaces. Outbreak racism is difficult to address because it is revolutionized with past and future fears that inchoately erupt and (re)surface. In this respect, the post-racial

> signifies . . . constantly shifting archipelagoes of technology, social arrangements, tacticalized legal and political regimes, channels of movement, all interpenetrating one another. This new social, political, economic and cultural configuration thus betrays a racism of interception. Unable to cement society together, racism organizes itself as a legitimate and justified self defense . . . It is a racism that is not so much organized on territoriality but much more directed towards mobility. (Valayden 2013, 155)

The itinerant other leads to a *racism of interception* that defends against existing and future threats. Valayden presents the incitement of building 'walls', such as between the U.S. and Mexico border, as exemplifying post-racial control. The making of 'real' and 'virtual' boundaries are more a biopolitical security response struggling to *manage* flows of the other, than efficacious practices of containment.

In the case of digital 'hashtag activism', the phenomena of *#BlackLives-Matter* and 'Black Twitter' have disrupted the imaginary whiteness of online spaces (Bonilla and Rosa 2015; Brock 2020; Sharma 2013). A key battleground, the Alt-Right was channelled towards a perpetual contestation of appropriating and usurping networks of communication. As an example, the 2014 protests against the fatal police shooting of Michael Brown in Ferguson (USA) were actively supported (both on- and off-line) by the #BlackLives-Matter movement. In response, the hashtag *#TCOT* (Top Conservatives on Twitter) – frequently linked to the Alt-Right's *#WhiteGenocide* (Wilson 2018) – was combatively deployed as a counter-narrative to displace and silence *#BlackLivesMatter* (Ray et al. 2017).

Bharath Ganesh (2020) points out that the Alt-Right 'captures the attention of its audiences and the forms of affect and emotion that it mobilizes are aspects . . . not well understood' (1). In response, I develop an account of the outbreak racism of the Alt-Right. Firstly, exploring how this racism is tied to a 'bio-political fascism that is all about the active liberation of certain political subjectivities/agencies at the expense of others' (Evans 2013, 60). And secondly, how the Alt-Right is constituted online as an amorphous 'crowd of contagion', which has been onerous to challenge.

Weaponizing Culture

Networked communications have flourished through *participatory* social media platforms. Popular sites such as Twitter, Facebook, YouTube, Reddit and 4Chan to varying degrees festered the online evolution of the Alt-Right. The Alt-Right has played a pivotal role in mainstreaming racism and normalizing neo-fascist convictions. If it had a game plan it has been to shift the 'Overton window' – making invidious ideas and feelings tolerable in the public realm (Daniels 2018; Wendling 2018). The Alt-Right has been relentless in articulating racist expression that edge towards greater acceptability. A plethora of tactics emerged to overturn the status-quo, which include drawing upon ideas from the revolutionary left. In particular, there is an influence of 'situationism', when the Alt-Right intervenes in the *cultural* sphere rather than only operating in the realm of politics (Marcy 2020). These activities were propelled by the (Gramscian-inspired) maxim, '*politics is downstream from culture*', as declared by Andrew Brietbart, founder of the notorious far-right website (Ebner 2019).

The attraction to the arena of culture by the Alt-Right has antecedents in how earlier fascist movements sought to manipulate feelings and mobilize

publics. When Walter Benjamin famously stated 'fascism as the aestheticiza-
tion of politics', he diagnosed how cultural technologies were deployed to
render politics as spectacle, consumption and entertainment while enabling
forms authoritarianism and ethno-nationalism (Koepnick 1999, 52). In the
digital age, the Alt-Right harnessed networked modes of communication,
appropriating cultural *forms* (memes, gifs, video) and *practices* (irony, satire,
flaming, trolling) to stifle and hijack equality debates, and lure 'ordinary'
users towards participating in white supremacist discourses (Ganesh 2020;
Marwick and Lewis 2017; Nagle 2017).

Understanding the aesthetics of Alt-Right politics should avoid only presenting fascism as a 'historically constituted regime . . . or incipient ideology'
as Evans and Reid (2013, 1) maintain, and instead it 'is as diffuse as the phenomenon of power itself'. It is from this perspective, I explore the networked
racial 'micro-fascism' of the Alt-Right and how it emerged online.

Deleuze and Guattari (1987) focus on micro-fascism that spreads through
the fabric of society, prior to its (macro- or 'molar') political organization.
They identify micropolitical forces of fascism that collectivize *desire*:

> fascism is inseparable from a proliferation of molecular forces of interaction,
> which skip from point to point, before beginning to resonate together . . . What
> makes fascism dangerous is its molecular or micropolitical power, for it is a
> mass movement: a cancerous body rather than a totalitarian organism (215).

Desire is productive, constantly breaking down limits and making connections, like a 'machine'. Desire is involved in the production of the social,
which emerges from desiring machines that dis/connect or break/flow
(Genosko 2017). These machines work as assemblages via connective flows.

Assemblages can be characterized as consisting of three kinds of 'flows'
or 'lines', as Luise de Miranda (2013) succinctly puts it: 'Desire makes
things flow, this is the *rupture* line [of flight]. Desire flows, this is the *molecular* line. Desire seizes up, this is the *molar* line' (132; emphasis added).
The molecular lines constantly shift and change. Their flows can give rise to
indeterminate intensities and affects, which can either be captured by molar
lines, or accelerated and freed by rupture lines of flight. In contrast, the flow
of desire is arrested by molar lines that territorialize and stratify. These lines
are prescriptive and organize assemblages – giving rise to meanings, representations and classifications, false and binary oppositions, hierarchical
social identities and all the way through to the formation of nation-states.

Rather than conceiving society as contestations of only molar formations,
the three lines of the molar, molecular and rupture-flight are interwoven.
The molecular can breakdown and exceed the molar, which is why Deleuze
and Guattari (1987) stress, '[f]rom the viewpoint of micro politics, a society
is defined by its lines of flight' (216).[11] When these lines 'fail' to escape, it

can lead to 'black-holes,' and 'every fascism is defined by a micro-black hole' (214). We can consider the force of a black hole as activating forms of *outbreak racism*, clamorous and raging, teeming with destructive affects and attachments.

A compelling expression of the racial micro-fascism of the Alt-Right was the meme of 'Pepe the Frog'. Created in 2005 by Matt Furiewhich, Pepe was an innocent cartoon-book character. The anthropomorphized frog began to circulate online, originally as the 'feels good, man' reaction image (an irreverent response by the frog peeing his pants) (Pettis 2019). Pepe's smile was then inverted and re-captioned as a 'feels bad, man' meme. As it continued to spread across the internet and remixed, the Pepe meme became associated with increasingly bizarre and offensive themes. Not long after, White nationalists picked up Pepe on a 4Chan imageboard, and it morphed into a 'Kill Jews, man' meme.

The transformation into a racist meme, lead to the Anti-Defamation League (ADL) ingloriously labelling Pepe as a 'hate symbol', sharing the same status as the Nazi Swastika and Ku Klux Klan burning cross (Pettis 2019). But what propelled Pepe the Frog towards mainstream notoriety was during the 2016 U.S. presidential elections. Hillary Clinton on her campaign website produced 'an explainer' denouncing the frog as 'a symbol associated with white supremacy' (Chan 2016) – a move which spectacularly back-fired and super-charged the Alt-Right's appropriation of the frog. The pinnacle of Pepe's transmogrification, was when the 'Can you stump the Trump' election campaign video brazenly depicted a cartoon version of Donald Trump with the head of Pepe.

Clinton's attempt to counter the mainstreaming of what became a white nationalist symbol is emblematic of inadvertently supplying more 'oxygen' to the Alt-Right, which resists denouncement and ferociously feeds on publicity and attention (Phillips 2018). Alt-Right memes are symptomatic of an *outbreak racism* which simultaneously lionizes transgressive incivility and abases a call-out culture of 'political correctness'. Moreover, Robert Topinka (2019) points out that Clinton's attempt to censure via an Alt-Right 'explainer' becomes trapped in trying to demystify the hidden meanings of Pepe. It confuses the apparent inscrutability of Alt-Right memes, for their actual *intractable post-racial* form. Alt-Right memes commonly operate 'through the digital media aesthetics of the "stream" . . . where the signalling of links in circulatory networks replaces symbolic representation' (Topinka 2019). Social media streams spawn connectivity and foment intensities and affects that wildly proliferate in networks. The meme's mutant aesthetic fester modalities of racism able to 'hide in the light'.

An outbreak racism of interception can also be found in the Alt-Right slogan '*It's OK to be White*' (IOTBW), which attempts to come across as an innocuous message while spurring a backlash politics of white victimhood (Ganesh 2020). IOTBW began as poster campaign devised on a notorious 4Chan imageboard in 2016, and then circulated across a number of U.S. states, including fliers found in schools and campuses (Wilson 2018). In a blog post by the ADL, it cites a Twitter user revealing the strategy of the trolling poster campaign designed to 'trigger' liberals and mainstream media:

> 'The point of IOTBW . . . is to bait shitlibs into showing their ass to normies. The beauty is in the simplicity . . . The next morning, the media goes completely berserk.' People would realize 'that leftists & journalists hate white people, so they turn on them.' This would . . . be a 'massive victory for the right in the culture war.' In addition, it would cause 'many more /ourguys/ [to be] spawned overnight'. (cited in ADL 2017)

Nevertheless, the ADL concludes the strategy as inherently flawed. They contend that publicly calling out the poster campaign as racist is justified, and would not be considered as anti-white. ADL point to some users circulating IOTBW as avowedly racist in their comments. And the slogan has long-standing connections with white supremacist groups. When the prominent white nationalist David Duke promoted IOTBW, ADL (2017) cites a 4Chan member lamenting 'I wish he stayed out of it'.

However, the IOTBW slogan *continued* to circulate and appear in prominent places. A T-Shirt emblazoned with the phrase is available to purchase on Amazon.com. IOTBW was remixed as an image meme in 2018, and taken up by a white supremacist candidate running for a congressional seat in Wisconsin, USA. The meme 'restages Martin Luther's nailing of the 95 Theses to the door of the Wittenberg Castle church. In this case, the thesis is that "It's Okay to Be White"' (Ganesh 2020, 16). In the same year, the Australian senate *narrowly* voted against a motion from the nativist One Nation party which proclaimed the 'deplorable rise of anti-white racism and attacks on Western civilisation' and that IOTBW is an acceptable statement (Karp 2018). As in the case of Clinton, the ADL misjudge how the Alt-Right *outbreak racism* overwhelms and resists its (historical) 'truth' being unmasked.

Gary Genosko (2017) highlights how the interminable trolling by the Alt-Right and the grotesque posturings, post-truths and racist tweets of its original figure-head Donald Trump, confounded being castigated as morally reprehensible or undermined by reason and evidence. The black hole effects of micro-fascisms suck and devour meanings, de-rail anti-racist critique and thwart progressive debate:

> The black hole both swallows up . . . racist and paranoid POTUS tweets . . . and spits out newly charged semiotic components that liberate the desire immanent

to the political landscape and make it resonate across the alt-right mediascape. (Genosko 2017, 64)

The mutability of networked cultural forms as they traverse through the affective circuits of white victimhood are charged by a *racism of interception*, that both provokes attention and spurns being called-out. Moreover, this racism can be devastating because it is often propagated by a 'swarming' of online users, connected by white rage and ressentiment.

Crowds and Contagion

The Alt-Right is routinely characterized – and *feared* – as an online 'crowd' or 'mob' able to rapidly mobilize to usurp debate, and relentlessly harass individuals and groups. Earlier studies of crowds by Gustave Le Bon, Elias Canetti and Gabriel Tarde explore how 'the crowd works according to a logic of contagion' (Stage 2013, 2). And in more recent analyses of online crowds, contagion is deployed to account for how social influence is transmitted in networked spaces (Mitchell 2012; Kucharski 2020). The aesthetic forms and practices of Alt-Right memes, trolling and flaming are contagious via their qualities of imitation, repetition and suggestion. The Alt-Right crowd is activated through collectivized feelings of rage, victimization and entitlement.

A crowd may directly involve Alt-Right protagonists, or create contagious conditions for other users to become part of an online 'swarm'. The notorious case of the 2014 #*Gamergate* hashtag 'campaign' pushed to silence female journalists and media critics in the online games industry by using brutalizing threats of doxing, rape and death from a wide range of hostile actors (Massanari 2017). In the 2017 UK general election campaign, the long-standing black female MP, Diane Abbot, was viciously targeted with misogynistic and racist online 'hate', receiving almost half of all abusive messages against women MPs (Dhrodia 2018). These forms of outbreak racism possesses a monstrous capability to seemingly spontaneously emerge as an 'acephalic swarm' – leaderless with no semblant organizational structure (Dean 2010; Ganesh 2020).

It is useful to briefly explore the characteristics of digital networks that foment raging online crowds. Strong emotions, especially anger, fear and disgust, have been found more likely to be shared and transmitted on social media platforms. Adam Kucharski (2021) points out that the mechanism of how events spread and crowds form vary, ranging from a 'broadcast' event (from a common source), to 'cascading' events (propagating person-to-person). Kucharski stresses that the epidemiological analogy of 'virality' describing contagious online events is limited (because they do not grow exponentially). Instead, online cascades are discovered to be more like 'stuttering outbreaks' that are complicated to predict (and due to degrees of randomness). This helps to account for why the networked outbreak racism of the Alt-Right can be difficult to anticipate and challenge.

The abstruse workings of the Alt-Right leads to condemning it as a capricious, raging social media mob threatening civility. But there is a danger of echoing earlier conservative thought, such as by the influential French psychologist Gustave Le Bon, who presents a revolutionary mass as an irrational and barbarous crowd jeopardizing the social order. Christian Borch (2009) draws attention to Le Bon promoting a (racialized) biopolitical programme: 'in order to prevent an evolutionary regression, which would endanger the entire population, it is crucial to combat the crowd and its contagious effects' (274). This line of reasoning excoriates the Alt-Right as an aberrant social phenomena, and undermines reckoning with the mainstreaming of the 'depth of feeling' when 'politics becomes infused by the logic of crowds' (Davies 2018, 10).

According to Jodi Dean (2010), social media platforms such as 'Twitter and Facebook are not just tools; they are manifestations of affective intensities associated with crowds' (209). More specifically, we need to understand how the Alt-Right as a *networked crowd* 'weaponizes affect' (Ganesh 2020). Characterizing the Alt-Right as an amorphous online crowd signals its boundless shape and size. Rather than perceiving a crowd as an aggregation of countless individuals or groupings, it can be conceived as a 'molecular mass' that eludes categorization between the one and the many (Brighenti 2010; Ganesh 2020). The molecular domain is where the phenomena of the crowd as an undulatory and proliferating collective force occurs. The crowd is designated by its expression, movement and encounters. Andrea Brighenti (2010) characterizes the crowd as having two dimensions: 'the dromological (composition of relative speeds and slownesses) and the affective (capacities of affecting and being affected)' (304).[12]

The dromological circuits of affect in the formation of crowds explains how the Alt-Right and the force of whiteness propagate in networks. It calls attention to race as an event: 'a particular spatiotemporal disciplining and charging of . . . bodies' (Saldanha 2007, 190). The dromology of whiteness involves bodies 'slowing down' and affectively clustering, leading to connections that stick and exclude other differences. This 'viscosity' of whiteness materializes as a racial formation when connections to power and privilege repeat and endure over time and space.

An amorphous Alt-Right does not express a hegemonic whiteness. Rather it emerged as a series of 'affective resonances, as force field of attachments' (Hook 2005), swarming in the networked spaces of digital communications. To put it another way, the intensity of the whiteness of the Alt-Right is produced by affects that connect users and spread feelings of fear and ressentiment through digital networks.

A lasting legacy of the Alt-Right is its exploitation of digital networks to build undulatory 'crowds' that have normalized the spread of racism, 'hate speech', conspiracy theories and dis-information on a huge scale. The Alt-Right's weaponization of networked connectivity should not be seen as exceptional or aberrant. Rather, it reveals how digital networks are far from neutral communication infrastructures. The dominance of Big Tech and the lack of effective regulation have festered an environment in which forms of networked racism continue to thrive.

The study of networks continues to receive attention, because they are complex and evolving, their architectures, affordances and use are shaped by dynamic social and technological forces. When we accept the non-neutrality of networks and inequality of networked connectivity, it opens up questions of power, participation and exclusion. That is, to grasp 'digital racism' involves acknowledging how networks distribute and concentrate power. This is in relation to the turbulent social and political contexts networks operate in, as well as their technical infrastructures.

I have highlighted how digital networks are critical to post-racial control expressed by forms of 'differential inclusion' and 'outbreak racism'. These are racisms that are not necessarily hierarchical in organizing difference, yet are capable of profoundly effecting the digital landscape. The hyper-connectivity of networks intersects with control as a mode of power proliferating difference only to regulate its disruptive potential. To understand the post-raciality of digital racism is to grapple with the seeming inescapability of networks.

NOTES

1. Part III offers a detailed discussion of the significance of 'power law' distributions concerning which information and content becomes visible on social media platforms. It also explores social media networks as 'complex systems' with emergent and unpredictable properties.

2. GAFAM profits are also accumulated in the Global South. Though they are being challenged by the rise of tech companies in China such as Baidu, Tencent, Alibaba and Xiaomi (BATX).

3. 'Accumulation by dispossession' is a concept developed by David Harvey (2007) to understand contemporary capitalism/neoliberalism. He argues that accumulation of profit has shifted from the exploitation of labour in production, to dispossession. Dispossession may occur through commodification or the privatization of public assets or land. In the case of 'digital dispossession', this can, for example, occur through how our personal data is commodified. For a useful account of the notion of digital or data dispossession, see Catherine Gray (2021).

4. Couldry and Mejias offer a far deeper analysis of dispossession than Zuboff. Furthermore, for a critique of Zuboff's analogy with indigenous exploitation, see Kafer (2019).

5. While not the focus on my study, it is important to acknowledge literature exploring decolonizing technology, especially from the Global South. For example, see Sahana Udupa and Ethiraj Gabriel Dattatreyan (2023).

6. In contrast to Foucault, Achille Mbembe's (2003) account of 'necropolitics' stresses the use of racial violence and death-making in the regulation and control of populations. And Weheliye (2014) criticizes Foucault's formulation of biopolitics for failing to take account of race vis-à-vis its colonial operations. Notwithstanding these elisions, Puar (2017) highlights how Foucault's account of biopolitics and security can be productively mined to grasp contemporary modalities of racism and control.

7. For a discussion of the 'post-racial' condition, see the Prologue.

8. It will become evident that 'Alt-Right' promotes a biopolitical racism predicated on disposability of racialized populations.

9. The Associated Press adopted the position not to use the term 'Alt-Right' to avoid enabling far right groups to define themselves. For the purpose of my argument with a focus on techno-politics, I continue to use the label 'Alt-Right', while acknowledging its self-aggrandizing status.

10. The problematic distinction between 'ordinary' and 'extreme' racism is explored in part III.

11. Deleuze and Guattari have been celebrated for wanting to activate lines of flight that *escape* (deterritorialize) through liberating desire; the potential of revolutionary social change, 'becomings' of creativity and new possibilities.

12. Brighenti develops an understanding of crowds by drawing on Elias Canetti, Gabriel Tarde and Giles Deleuze.

Part II

Algorithms

'*Fuck the Algorithm*!' was chanted outside the Department of Education, London, in August 2020. Perhaps for the first time at a public protest an algorithm was singled out – for wrecking the life-chances of thousands of students. During the COVID-19 pandemic, 'A'-Level examinations, used to determine university places, were withdrawn by the Conservative government. As an alternative, the Office of Qualifications and Examinations Regulation (Ofqual) deployed an algorithm to determine student grades. It was a spectacular failure. Up to 40 percent of students received lower grades than expected – downgraded from what teachers had predicted, leading to students losing their university places, and threats of legal action against the government. The incumbent prime minister, Boris Johnson witlessly defended the 'objectivity' of the algorithm producing 'robust' and 'dependable' standardized results (Coughlan 2020). A huge public outcry led to a humiliating government climb-down over the use of a flawed algorithm.

The Royal Statistical Society (RSS) had raised concerns about Ofqual's algorithm a month before its launch. How Ofqual's algorithm predicted grades is complicated. Ofqual released a report consisting of a voluminous 319 pages that presented a detailed account of the algorithm (Stockford 2020). This should come as no surprise, as the majority of algorithms deployed to automate decisions are dependent on mathematics (statistical models) beyond public understanding, or the algorithms are propriety (protected by trade secrets), or opaque by design (e.g. 'machine learning' algorithms). The renowned software engineer and consultant, Jeni Tennison (2020) CEO of the Open Data Institute, produced an impressive online explainer of Ofqual's model. Nevertheless, Tennison admits that Ofqual's report is an 'arduous read in places' and includes her own disclaimer: 'understanding of what they've done may not always be accurate!'[1]

Ofqual's focus was on schools rather than individual students. The algorithm used the distribution of grades from previous years to assign grades to students in rank order.[2] Although, for schools submitting small cohorts of students, teacher-predicted grades were used. This had the effect of disproportionately boosting grades for independent (fee-charging) schools, who traditionally enter smaller cohort sizes than state-supported schools. Moreover, student cohort size can act as a proxy for educational inequities. Smaller cohort sizes are more likely to represent white and/or class-privileged students attending independent schools. The proportion of 'A' grades awarded to independent schools was more than double the rate for state schools (Adams and McIntyre 2020).

Ofqual's algorithm did not explicitly include variables related to race or ethnicity for predicting grades. Nonetheless, ethno-racial disparities – that is, institutional and structural forms of racism – are manifest throughout the educational pipeline. In particular, making algorithmic predictions of grades based on *historical data* deepened extant inequities and embedded patterns of racial discrimination in the student selection process for university places (cf. Kizilcec and Hansol 2021).

Over the last decade, there has been a rapid deployment of computer-based algorithms across society. They have become embedded in automating decision-making in areas of education and employment, health and welfare, housing, policing, criminal justice and surveillance. Algorithms are also extensively used for commercial data-mining and advertising, recommendation systems (web search, online shopping surveillance) and dynamic pricing (e.g. for booking transport services). Algorithms underpin AI 'self-learning' systems in developing driver-less vehicles, speech recognition and online conversational agents.

Notably, there's been a shift towards using the expression 'AI' (Artificial Intelligence) over the term 'algorithm'. An algorithm is basically an instruction set, a sequence of steps to follow to solve a problem. The sequence could be a simple set of IF-THEN statements or involving more complex mathematical equations to build a statistical model. It is in the realm of computation and statistics that algorithms marshal their analytical power. The roots of the concept of an algorithm can be traced to famed ninth-century-mathematician Muḥammad ibn Mūsā al-Khwārizmī, who highlighted that numbers can solve worldly problems. His Latinised name, al-Khwārizmī, derives the term 'algoritmi'.

Algorithms are at the centre of AI systems. The term 'Artificial Intelligence' was coined by the computer scientist John McCarthy in the 1950s (a founder of AI labs at MIT and Stanford). Early forms of AI were 'symbolic' or 'rule-based' (pre-programmed by humans), and largely failed to deliver the promise of being able to intelligently solve real-world problems (such as computer vision or speech recognition). This form of AI is being super-seded by 'connectionist' or 'machine learning', dependent on 'big data' and computing power (Katz 2020). Instead of being pre-programmed, machine-learning algorithms are trained on copious amounts of data, producing 'mod-els' which are then applied to process new data inputs to make decisions or predictions.[3] These systems are said to 'learn' from the training data. They are being developed as 'generative AI' capable of autonomously producing outputs; for instance, using 'artificial neural network' architectures to detect unknown patterns in disparate types of data and generate new inferences.

There is prodigious hype over what AI can achieve – what some critics scathingly call out 'AI snake-oil' (Kapoor and Narayanan 2022). In the future it is claimed that entirely autonomous machine-learning models will lead to human-like, so-called Artificial General Intelligence (AGI). AI is a vague, obfuscatory term; and as with most computing technologies, its formation lies in the military-industrial-academic complex (Katz 2020). My focus will be on machine-learning algorithms as the object of analysis.

The belief that algorithms are neutral, objective or fair in their social impact has been progressively challenged. While there are long-standing cri-tiques against computer-based automated forms of decision-making, ground-breaking books such as Cathy O'Neil (2016) *Weapons of Maths Destruction*, Virginia Eubanks (2018) *Automating Inequality* and Safiya Noble (2018) *Algorithms of Oppression* promoted the need for a critical and public under-standing of the inequitable impacts of algorithms, especially against margin-alized and vulnerable populations. These texts revealed how algorithms are part of daily life, but remain largely hidden and unregulated in their opera-tions against the most marginalized in society. A central feature of this work exposed the impact of algorithms and how inequality and racism are 'baked-in' automated decision-making systems of both Big Tech and the state.

It is difficult to keep track of the spiralling incidents of AI or algorithmic 'bias' and discriminatory impacts being studied or publicly reported. A cursory web search for the query 'algorithms are racist' to date, yields over three million results. Concerns over AI harms have gained ascendancy across civil society, government and corporate sectors. Nonetheless, how issues of potential discriminatory algorithms are grasped, and the possible 'solutions' put forward, are divergent and seemingly discordant. Take for example, the widespread aim to develop 'fairer' and 'unbiased' algorithms. It remains con-testable what 'fairness' or 'bias' might be (Hanna et al. 2020), and fundamen-tally, how the object of the algorithm should be conceived (Dourish 2016). Due to the absence of common points of reference, discussing algorithmic or AI bias in a meaningful way is challenging. To introduce some clarity, three positions can be distinguished to navigate debates over 'algorithmic bias' and what is also referred to as 'AI Ethics'.

Firstly, a 'techno-solutionist' perspective (Morozov 2014) promotes a technical 'fix' (e.g. improving datasets and/or algorithmic models) to overcome the problem of bias. Secondly, a 'fairness' approach aims at improving AI systems via auditing for discriminatory effects, and calls for transparency, accountability and regulation (including a turn towards 'explainable AI'). Thirdly, 'critical', 'data justice' and 'abolitionist' perspectives firmly situate algorithms as part of wider sociotechnical assemblages that are governed by systemic forms of oppression.

The fairness approach – exemplified by the influential Association for Computing Machinery (ACM) Conference 'Fairness, Accountability, and Transparency' (FAT, renamed as FAccT) – has gained most traction in addressing algorithmic bias. More recently, its position appears to be shifting towards engaging with elements of data justice perspectives. Similarly, the prominent Neural Information Processing Systems Conference (NeurIPS 2023) has made it mandatory for conference submissions to address 'any potential negative societal impacts'. This shift is also reflected in the emergence of a plethora of groups interrogating and campaigning against automated social harms, including *Black in AI, AINow, Algorithmic Justice League, Data & Society, Algorithmic Watch* and *DataActive*.

However, fairness and critical approaches in relation to the design of algorithmic systems are evidently having minimal impact. In a revealing study, Abeba Birhane et al. (2021) analysed the '*values*' propagated in the most influential (highly cited) machine-learning papers published in premier computing conferences of the International Conference on Machine Learning (ICML) and NuerIPS. These publications were discovered to be dominated by Big Tech corporations and elite universities that privilege *technical* issues of performance, optimization and efficiency; and largely neglect the risk of algorithms perpetuating social inequalities.

There has been an institutionalization of techno-solutionism via the rise of a duplicitous AI discourse of corporate responsibility, which arguably is no more than an 'ethics-washing' smokescreen for 'business-as-usual' in the pursuit of hyper-connectivity and monetizing user engagement (Nachtwey and Seidl 2020). And on the pretext of state securitization, there has been an expansion of regimes of algorithmic surveillance as manifested by the intensification of predictive policing, pre-emptive counter-terrorism and border security. Much of these developments are abnegating problems of racialized profiling and exclusions produced by systems of control (Amoore 2021; Sharma and Nijjar 2018, 2023; Wang 2018).

Continuing the argument presented in part I, I develop an understanding of algorithms as *post-racial technologies of control*. This does not dwell on demonstrating whether algorithms are involved in entrenching social harm. There is burgeoning research and countless examples evidencing the discriminatory impacts of algorithms on marginalized groups. Nonetheless, to declare that algorithms are 'biased' or they propagate forms of 'algorithmic racism' should prompt us to consider how algorithms are being conceived and what kind of agency they exhibit.

I explore the limits of understanding automated oppression and violence when characterized as algorithmic *bias*. These accounts implicitly present algorithms or AI as 'black boxed' in relation to how 'bias' is either a bug or a flaw located in the algorithm's code. It gives rise to techno-solutionist positions attesting that algorithms as stable and singular objects can be 'fixed' and 'de-biased'. In opposition, critical-data studies perspectives contend there is no simple fix, and locate the problem of 'bias' (i.e. social harm) as existing throughout wider iniquitous social systems that algorithmic assemblages are part of. I share and advance critical-abolitionist perspectives, and maintain grasping algorithms as assembled beyond their black-boxed characterization.

Nonetheless, there is a possibility that by moving too quickly to focus on the systemic consequences of algorithmic harm we ignore the post-racial 'agency' of algorithms, and inadvertently reinforce their black-boxed inscriptions. When students protested against Ofqual, it was not merely a reification of the algorithm to direct rage against automating educational injustice. The chant centred on how algorithms – insipidly presented as neutral technical objects – embody and *generate* forms of discrimination and exclusion. To put it another way, from a Science and Technology Studies (STS) perspective, black boxes are the carriers of social relations (Biker et al. 2012). And to continue, as Benjamin (2017) maintains, we can consider racism 'as a set of technologies that generate patterns of social relations, and these become Black-boxed as natural, inevitable, automatic' (44–45).

The agency of algorithms is examined in terms of their generative 'race-making' capacities. This is not a revelatory attempt to look inside the black box of algorithms, but to identify what algorithms *do* in relation to enacting modalities of techno-racism. In an age of in/security, algorithms are being deployed 'in which social problems are made conceivable only as objects of calculative control' (Hong 2022, 2). More specifically, I interrogate how algorithms *mobilize logics of post-raciality* by obfuscating transformations of racism via computational technologies (cf. Kafer 2019). Contemporary examples of policing and counter-terror surveillance are highlighted, to analyse how *predictive* machine-learning algorithms are fundamental to enacting post-racial technologies of calculative control.

WHAT BIAS?

In 2020 a team of researchers from Duke University (Menon et al. 2020) presented a paper called 'PULSE' at the Computer Vision and Pattern

Recognition (CVPR) conference, one of the largest annual AI events in the world. The paper demonstrated an innovative photo recreation model – combining 'self-supervised' machine learning with a generative adversarial network – which produced high-quality realistic facial images of people from low-resolution, pixelated images. However, when released to wider community of researchers, it did not take long to discover that the PULSE computer vision model preformed dismally when input with images of people of colour. For instance, pixelated photos of Barack Obama and Alexandria Ocasio-Cortez were rendered into high-resolution figures who appeared phenotypically 'white'.

These unsettling images were circulated on Twitter and swiftly admonished for exemplifying racial 'bias' in machine learning. In an explanatory (defensive) tweet, Yann LeCun wrote:

> ML systems are biased when data is biased. This face upsampling system makes everyone look white because the network was pretrained on FlickFaceHQ, which mainly contains white people pics. Train the *exact* same system on a dataset from Senegal, and everyone will look African (LeCun 2020a)

LeCun, a professor at New York University and chief scientist at Meta (Facebook) is a lauded figure in computer vision research. He is considered a founder of convolutional neural networks (CNN) and has been described as a 'godfather' of 'AI' and 'deep learning' (Vincent 2019). In his Twitter profile, LeCun highlights his ACM Turing Award Laurette, which is recognized as the '"highest distinction in computer science" and "Nobel Prize of Computing"' (Heidelberg Laureate Forum).

In his tweet, LeCun contends that the problem of 'bias' principally lies with the Flickr Face HQ (FFHQ) *data set* (compiled by Nvidia researchers in 2017) used by the PULSE model. The model performed well when transforming pixelated 'white' faces because the training dataset predominantly consisted of this grouping. LeCun frames the issue by echoing the classic computing problem of 'garbage in, garbage out': regardless of how accurate an algorithm is at processing data, the quality of its outputs is fundamentally determined by the quality of its inputs.

In response to LeCun, Timnit Gebru tweeted:

> I'm sick of this framing. Tired of it. Many people have tried to explain, many scholars. Listen to us. You can't just reduce harms caused by ML to dataset bias. (Gebru 2020a)

Gebru, is a leading research scientist exploring the problems of computer vision and racial bias. She co-developed (alongside MIT Media Lab researcher,

Joy Buolamwini) the project 'Gender Shades' which revealed the lack of accuracy of commercial facial recognition software with respect to darker-skinned people, especially women. The project influenced U.S. lawmakers to call for the halt of using this technology in federal government, and appeared to sway some Big Tech companies such as Microsoft and Amazon to end selling this software to law enforcement agencies. Gebru also co-founded the *Black in AI* group, advocating for greater diversity and inclusion in the field of AI. More recently, she is a founder of *Distributed Artificial Intelligence Research Institute* (DAIR), which works with AI researchers across the world.

Gebru was a co-lead of Google's ethical AI-team until the company forced her out in 2020. She co-authored a research paper 'On the Dangers of Stochastic Parrots: Can Language Models Be Too Big?' (Bender et al. 2021), highlighting ostensible risks associated with Large Language Models (LLM) and strategies required to mitigate these risks. The development of large-scale Natural Language Processing (NLP) is a vital computational enterprise for Big Tech (e.g. deployed in search engines, sentiment analysis of social media, voice assistants, chatbots and spam filters). Google opposed the publication of the paper in its original form, which effectively led to Gebru's position being terminated. The debacle over her role at Google lays bare the tensions between critical perspectives against the rise of imperious corporate AI Ethics.

Gebru's response to LeCun triggered a lengthy back-and-forth Twitter thread, generating a huge number of replies and thousands of likes and retweets. Followers of both protagonists piled into an increasingly polarized and acrimonious debate. Gebru's frustration is with LeCun reductively locating the problem of algorithmic harm to only 'bias' in the dataset. She points to her video tutorials about the problems of fairness and ethics at the CVPR 2020 conference which stress that it is not enough to call for more 'diverse datasets', while ignoring 'social and structural problems'. And Gebru continues in a follow-up tweet:

> Even amidst of world wide protests people don't hear our voices and try to learn from us, they assume they're experts in everything. Let us lead her[e] and you follow. Just listen. And learn from scholars like @ruha9 [Ruha Benjamin]. We even brought her to your house, your conference (Gebru 2020b).

Gebru makes reference to Benjamin's (2020) keynote address urging for a 'historically and sociologically grounded approach' towards critically assessing AI systems, at the International Conference on Learning Representations (ICLR) – of which LeCun is the president.

LeCun defends his tweet by subsequently declaring that it was to merely draw attention to the problem of bias in datasets as in the specific case of

PULSE, and highlights his awareness of more general problems of fairness with AI systems. While attempting to elaborate his position, LeCun eventually signs off the Twitter thread, blaming the animosity of the exchanges, and pleads that users stop attacking Gebru *and* himself. Such a hollow conciliatory gesture elides how the hostility against LeCun is hardly comparable to the targeted racialized and gendered attacks against Gebru. Black researchers such as Gebru are routinely vilified as being part of a woke, SJW crowd pushing to censure eminent AI practitioners. In a follow-up post on Facebook, LeCun makes reference to being lectured on 'the linguistic codes of social justice' in the Twitter thread. He claims not to be 'tone policing'[4] while simultaneously declaring it 'makes me fear for the future of rational discourse' (LeCun 2020b).

One of the characteristics of 'liberal' AI practitioners is to claim an objective, enlightened perspective, which denies and is oblivious to occupying a speaking position of white authority. Take for example a supporter of LeCun, the AI researcher John Stokes (2021) – recipient of a prestigious MIT Banting Fellowship. The viewpoint expressed by Stokes is worth scrutinizing, as it is exemplary for revealing the *post-racial* logics of AI.

The lengthy and detailed articles appearing on the popular Substack blogging platform by Stokes defend the probity of mainstream ML applications, while appearing to acknowledge concerns raised by critical AI researchers. He writes,

> AI/ML has real problems, and real potential for widespread harm. The AI ethics folks have at times pointed out real issues that demand urgent attention, and I credit them with bringing these things to light in a way that has caused many of us to begin focusing on them.

Yet at the same time he denounces Gebru as part of a politicized 'AI ethics rage mob', which has the effect of undermining critical perspectives and legitimizing a supposedly balanced AI ethics discourse.

Stokes, who has no credible background in analysing issues of social inequality, does exactly what Gebru accuses the mainstream AI research community of doing: '[they] don't hear our voices and try to learn from us, they assume they're experts in everything.' Stokes's antipathy to the *politics* of critical/data justice perspectives is symptomatic of a deeper *post-racial* logic that promotes the neutrality of computational systems vis-à-vis valorizing their technical (mathematical) operations, while proffering accounts of algorithmic 'bias' that occlude the impact of systemic inequities. Stokes exploits the discourse of a burgeoning field of AI Ethics, which lacks a settled understanding of what *bias* is and where it is located in machine-learning systems.

In attempting to address the concern of 'bias', David Danks and Alex London (2017) suggest conceiving it *non-pejoratively*: '"bias" simply refers to deviation from a standard. Thus, we can have statistical bias in which an estimate deviates from a statistical standard (e.g. the true population value); moral bias in which a judgment deviates from a moral norm' (4692). They maintain the importance of distinguishing between different types of bias, because not all are detrimental. This type of intervention appears helpful in calling for greater precision when discussing bias in AI systems. Although, we shall discover that bifurcating algorithmic bias as an inevitable *technical property* of statistical operations versus bias as mode of *social harm* can lead to post-racial obfuscations of carceral power and control. When situating machine-learning systems as sociotechnical assemblages, their operations cannot be divorced from how they are entangled with societal forms of oppression (Lee et al. 2019; McQuillan 2022).

Harini Suresh and John Guttag (2021) take up the challenge of advancing a more expansive understanding of algorithmic bias. They map how discriminatory processes are embedded in machine-learning systems, by presenting a framework for identifying when and how 'bias' (sociotechnical harms) arise in a machine-learning pipeline (see figure 2.1). Their work is worth elaborating, because it is a rare example of demystifying how multiple modalities of bias occur in practice.

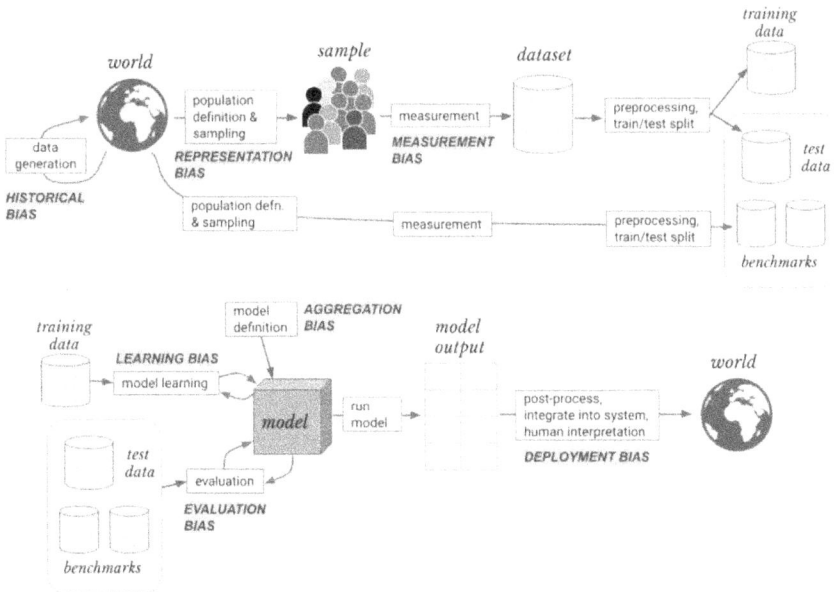

Figure 2.1   Machine Learning Pipeline.

Suresh and Guttag begin with an overview of a machine learning life cycle, summarized in three stages:

(a) *Data Generation* compiles a *dataset* identifying 'a target population of people or things', and including 'measuring features and labels'. The data may be labelled, unlabelled or a mixture. The dataset is usually split into training data and test data for the next stage.

(b) *Model Development* refers to the dataset used to build a *model*. A model comprises developing a machine learning (prediction) algorithm run on the training data.[5] 'Typically, models are trained to optimize a specified objective, such as minimizing the . . . error between its prediction and the actual labels' (2). Simply put, the model 'learns' from the training data, which are used to make classifications or predictions on new data inputs. The model is evaluated with the test data, and its performance may also be checked against benchmark datasets.

(c) *Model Output* presents appropriate outputs of the model, such as using risk score and visualize its results for stakeholders and regulatory agencies. The model may require documentation indicating the explainability of its outputs.

After outlining the machine learning life cycle, Suresh and Guttag delineate a taxonomy of potential sources of harm.[6] This offers a nuanced account of machine learning bias beyond 'vague terms like "algorithmic bias" or "data bias"' (4). Sources of harm are located in relation to the three stages of the ML pipeline.

'Historical', 'Representation' and 'Measurement' forms of bias are associated with the first stage of Data Generation. Historical bias can appear intangible in how it is manifested in algorithms. It may accumulate over time, over-determining how an object or identity comes to be known. For example, how the behaviour of a group becomes racialized (and expressed via stereotypes), or how certain categories or expressions in language become charged by race and associated with particular discriminatory meanings. This kind of enduring accretive 'bias' is arguably the most significant because it situates computational processes as systems that can be integral to modes of societal oppression. Regardless of how accurately data is measured and sampled, historical bias can lead to a model producing social harm. It is this type of 'bias' that critical-data justice approaches increasingly call attention to (beyond merely bad datasets), when highlighting how systemic oppressions are elemental to automated decision-making systems, and are historically 'baked-in' to the machine-learning pipeline.

A key form of Representational bias is evident when the target population of a dataset does not adequately reflect the diversity of the wider population.

In the case of the PULSE model, it implemented the Face StyleGAN model trained on the Flickr Face HQ dataset that was found to be dominated by faces of white subjects (Menon et al. 2020). It is usually this reference to 'biased data' that AI researchers, such as LeCun, exalt when promoting solutions for ML bias. However, *occluded* in these accounts is sufficiently acknowledging related historical and measurement forms of bias. In the latter case, this refers to the challenge of selecting and computing features and labels used for prediction. And these features or labels often act as proxies for phenomena not directly measurable. For example, for risk assessment in the criminal justice system, 'data for models like these often include proxy variables such as "arrest" to measure "crime" or some underlying notion of "riskiness". Because minority communities are more highly policed, this proxy is differentially mismeasured' (Suresh and Guttag 2021, 5).

'Aggregation', 'Learning' and 'Evaluation' bias are associated with the second stage of Model Development. It is these specific types of bias which are routinely conflated in accounts attempting to discuss 'algorithmic bias'. Aggregation bias surfaces when a 'one-size-fits-all' model is developed for data which represents different groups or norms. '[It] can lead to a model that is not optimal for any group, or a model that is fit to the dominant population (e.g., if there is also representation bias)' (5). For example, an automated Natural Language Processing (NLP) model for moderating offensive content on social media platforms may censor racialized terms expressed in anti-racist commentary.

A preeminent feature of automated decision-making systems is their capacity to 'learn'. However, Learning bias arises in machine-learning when a model *amplifies* 'performance disparities on data with under-represented attributes' (6), which can result in only the most frequent features being recognized. Many machine-learning algorithms are designed to *optimize* a function, for instance, this can be for encoding a measure of accuracy. But if overall accuracy is prioritized over another objective, it can lead to excessive false positives, such as Muslim civilians mis-identified as terrorists by pre-emptive state security surveillance (Munk 2017).

The development of a machine-learning algorithm is based on its training data. To check the quality of the model involves assessing it in relation to an established external dataset, referred to as a benchmark. 'Evaluation bias occurs when the benchmark data used for a particular task does not represent the use population' (Suresh and Guttag 2021, 6). The problem is that prominent and commercial benchmark datasets lack accountability in their production. Take for example the influential ImageNet benchmark dataset for visual object recognition; it includes limited representations of minoritized groups and relies on inconsistent crowd-sourced labelling of images (Denton et al. 2021). This can produce a model that mis-leadingly appears to perform well against its benchmark. Yet in practice, a model's success is specific to the accurately represented subgroups in the benchmark dataset, while obscuring its under-performance for other poorly represented subgroups.

The Model Output is the last stage of the ML cycle, and this is where 'Deployment bias' can occur. This leads to incongruities between the intended problem a model is designed for, and its actual deployment (also known as an 'alignment' problem). It points to how automated decision-making machine-learning models are not fully autonomous technical systems operating in isolation. As an example, Suresh and Guttag highlight the problem of how algorithmic risk assessments are deployed in criminal justice systems. These models are designed to (dubiously) predict the possibility of a future crime being committed, though in practice they are also being misused to determine the length of incarceration.

Stokes (2021) acknowledges the machine-learning pipeline diagram (figure 2.1) for distinguishing different types of bias. However, he occludes almost all its points of bias as inconsequential, and accuses critical AI researchers of guilelessly conflating and confounding social concerns with technical issues. Understanding how Stokes characterizes 'bias' reveals how it is derailed and emptied of any critical purchase, particularly through a framing of algorithmic systems as 'black boxes'.

By dismissing radical AI Ethics as unconscionably politicized by Critical Race Theory – duty-bound to invoke the inexhaustibly of racialized structural oppression, according to Stokes – he wantonly casts aside the enduring force of 'historical' bias in the ML pipeline. Stokes limits his attention to aggregation and evaluation bias (referred to as algorithmic or model bias). He contends that 'algorithmic bias' is a key *target* for critical AI proponents because this type of bias functions as an automated decision-making 'black box' that most people have no control over, and its inner mathematical workings are beyond their comprehension. And because of this, he presents an elementary algorithmic sorting example to unveil, in his words, 'the alchemy that lets an AI ethicist turn a bit of math into "racism"'.

Stokes's example consists of presenting a group of ten balls, five white, four black and one grey, and the task is to represent the collection with only one ball with a single colour. Two common ball sorting schemes are identified. Firstly, by averaging the colours of the ball weighted by the number of balls of that colour. This results in a single ball of a greyish colour, which only closely resembles the one grey ball in the collection. Secondly, selecting the most frequent colour in the collection results in a white ball being chosen, even though white balls only make up half the group. By substituting the balls for people and their skin colours, Stokes highlights that in either scheme, the 'black people' will be erased.

The simple example is meant to illuminate the most elementary operations machine-learning models perform. That is, such models are likely to 'discriminate' against outliers or phenomena that appear on the margins. Stokes maintains that many of these models essentially rely on statistical techniques that are inescapably 'biased' or 'unfair' in their *mathematical* operations by suppressing one set of data points and amplifying another. And when these are applied to datasets characterizing human populations, namely marginalized or under-represented groups, Stokes asserts that AI critics disingenuously insist that black-boxed algorithms racially discriminate against minorities:

> an implementation engineer will run some human-derived data . . . and find that the model is 'biasing' the results along race/gender/etc. lines. And whenever this happens, a conference paper can be written about that problem and added to the literature on 'algorithmic bias,' where it will eventually make its way into tweets, talks, and books about how algorithms themselves can be inherently racist independent of the input data. (Stokes 2022)

Alongside LeCun, Stokes occupies a 'liberal' position, which as we have observed appears to acknowledge potential detrimental impacts of unfair automated decision-making. Nonetheless, his dismissal of almost all the forms of bias highlighted in the machine-learning pipeline (figure 2.1) is at odds with such purported awareness of the social harms of AI. The ball sorting example enables Stokes to claim how the inherent *technical* functioning of algorithmic models – *not racism!* – is what needs to be grasped by critics of AI.

In opposition to perspectives challenging the deployment of AI in unjust societies, liberal AI researchers, maintain that bias or unfairness in ML systems is ultimately '*fixable*'. Such accounts are predicated on transforming complex manifestations of social inequality and difference into metrics. As Dan McQuillan (2022) contends, these lead to conceiving fairness 'as a mathematical distribution of benefits or harms. But, in the end, the root problem is seeing the computation as the structure that needs fixing rather than the structure of society itself' (34). To put it another way, the techno-solutionist perspective of 'fixable' (and explainable) AI is symptomatic of an insidious post-racial logic that elides – or we can say, '*black boxes*' (Benjamin 2019) – the problem of difference and racism in prevailing discourses of AI ethics.

The Black Box Problem

Characterizing AI as a 'black box' has become a common line of critique against the opaqueness of machine-learning systems. What is less discussed is that the origin of the term dates back to the emergence of cybernetics – a positivist theory of rationalization, automation and *control* – closely tied to the rise of electronic warfare during the mid-twentieth century. The ideology of cybernetics seeks to overcome disorder and uncertainty (Hilgers 2011; Wang 2018). Cybernetics is concerned with understanding how a complex system behaves and interacts (via feedback loops) in relation to its environment. The components of a system are modelled as a black box because contrary to the enlightenment belief of transparency leading to knowledge, in the modern era, the opacity of a system does not necessarily inhibit its efficacy. The internal workings or contents of the black box need not be entirely known or observable. The focus is placed on the relationship between the inputs and outputs – 'to discern patterns of behaviour' for control (Murray 2012, 902).

Black boxing has become a metaphor and a practice for increasingly complex societies that manifestly engages with opacity, uncertainty and risk – grappling with (though not over-coming) the limits of not-knowing (Galloway 2012; Hilgers 2011). Phillip von Hilgers refers to the black box as an 'epistemic object', and writes: 'The call for transparency in our society is for this reason just one side of the coin, as no other society produces to such an extent the same sort of opacities of sheer technological complexity that the black box renders manageable' (54).

AI is characterized as a black box because it has appropriated the cybernetic assumption that the opaqueness of the innards of a complex system can indeed be a productive design feature (and not a bug). An exemplary case is a branch of machine-learning called 'deep learning', prized for its universal and autonomous capacity to 'intelligently' address complex tasks. Deep learning is being actively developed for applications at scale, such as image and facial recognition systems, speech recognition and driverless cars. This type of machine learning can be trained to discover hidden patterns – far beyond the capacity of humans – from huge and diverse sets of input data by using artificial neural networks. Contemporary neural networks (discussed below) are opaque by design, and currently, their predictive accuracy is traded against their explainability. The developers designing these systems are unable to reverse engineer and *comprehend* the 'machine reasoning' behind how deep learning models produce their results. As machine learning models become increasingly complex (size of training data/parameters), they produce unexpected outputs – characterized as 'emergent' properties (Ornes 2023) – which cannot be explained or anticipated by the designers of these systems.

The consequences of the opacity of predictive machine reasoning become significant in relation to how these decision-making systems are presented. That is, if an algorithm produces unexpected results or outputs that are socially discriminatory, the *black box problem* is invariably highlighted. For instance, Google image search disastrously mis-labelling pictures of black people as 'gorillas' (Noble 2018) was largely framed as an issue with the lack of transparency of the inner workings of the machine-learning algorithm and naive software engineers failing to grasp why these erroneous (racist) outputs were being generated.

As predictive AI systems continue to be rolled out, critiques against and responses to a 'black box society' made inscrutable by computational technologies have gained traction (Pasquale 2015). However, when AI or algorithmic models are epistemologically characterized as black boxes, they collide with the Enlightenment impetus of connecting visibility and transparency with knowledge and certainty (Ananny and Crawford 2018). In contrast, the post-Enlightenment cybernetic conception of the black-boxed algorithm exists in conditions of complexity and uncertainty, operating as a 'strategic unknown, enabling knowledge to be deflected and obscured' (Bucher 2018, 56). Notions of *biased* black-boxed algorithms lead to masking 'the multitude of relations algorithms are part of and produce', and which is 'linked to an objectivist understanding of how knowledge is produced' (Lee et al. 2019, 2).

A limited focus on uncovering the biases of algorithms can fail to address how racism is being activated by and through algorithmic *systems*. Thus, regardless of the simplicity of the ball sorting example presented by Stokes, his ersatz AI expertise peers *inside* the black box – rather than the assemblages it is part of – to reveal and make algorithmic bias explainable as a statistical inevitability. Stokes in effect makes a *post-racial* move of defining 'bias' which sidesteps the 'historical legacies of racial arrangement and injustice' (Goldberg 2015, 20).[7]

Critical perspectives of AI are aware that the biased 'black box' metaphor operates as a 'red herring' (Bucher 2018), and their focus has been re-directed towards interrogating how algorithms are integrated into *wider* social processes. Mike Ananny and Kate Crawford (2018) maintain that calls for greater transparency of algorithms render only one part of the system visible, and stress we need to 'hold systems accountable by looking across them' (974). This involves grappling with the entanglement of human and non-human assemblages, which cannot be limited to analysing code and data. Algorithmic systems are composed of 'institutionally situated code, practices, and norms with the power to create, sustain, and signify relationships among people and data through minimally observable, semiautonomous action' (Ananny 2016, 93).

Drawing on the relational ontologies of materialism and STS, critical AI perspectives conceive the agency of technical objects as *distributed* across the systems they are constituted by. It is from this standpoint that Francis Lee (2021) forcefully contends: 'Instead of analysing the racist algorithm we should be looking at racist assemblages – and where the possibility for agency, choice, and power reside in these assemblages' (67).

Moving beyond narrowly conceiving algorithms as biased black boxes relaying racism, yields significant critical impact in deconstructing the distribution of social harm of AI. Nonetheless, there is a possibility that making systems accountable can lose sight of analysing *emergent algorithmic* modalities of racializing power. And paradoxically, we may reinscribe black-boxed reasoning, as knowledge of the operations of algorithms is not considered necessary to adjudge their role in propagating social harm. Alternatively, the 'accountability' of algorithmic assemblages can be studied at different scales. Widening our analytical lens to examine algorithmic systems should not mean ignoring algorithmic generativity. When the data scientist, Cathy O'Neil (2020) starkly declares 'Algorithms are racist because we are racist', it prompts questions of the accountability and 'agency' of algorithms. We know that algorithms can be a conduit and amplifier of extant forms of societal racism. Though, what is more challenging to grasp is how they are also generative of new post-racial forms of techno-racism.

Louise Amoore, in her book *Cloud Ethics* (2020), advances an alternative standpoint – rethinking accountability – by centring the ethicopolitical call for algorithms to 'give accounts of the conditions of their emergence' (9). She diagnoses the problem of so-called black-boxed algorithms by stressing there is 'no outside' to situate, judge and remedy algorithmic decision-making:

> the rise of algorithmic power in society has been overwhelmingly understood as a problem of opaque and illegible algorithms infringing or undercutting a precisely legible world of rights belonging to human subjects. [. . .] To call for the opening of the black box, for transparency and accountability, then, is to seek to institute arrangements that are good, ethical, and normal, and to prevent the transgression of societal norms by the algorithm. (2020, 5)

Only seeking accountability of algorithms to regulate possible social harms or to 'de-bias' and eliminate their suspect 'values', forecloses coming to terms with how algorithms are actively *intervening* in an existing, unjust world replete with ethicopolitical contestations. A critical concern is how contemporary algorithms 'are not so much transgressing settled societal norms as establishing new patterns of good and bad, new thresholds of normality and abnormality, against which actions are calibrated' (6). Through this framing of the generative capacities of algorithms, I will explore how predictive algorithms are mobilizing post-racial logics of control.

PREDICTION

The most lauded property of AI is the ability to learn to classify and make decisions. How this is achieved is based on intensive computational processes and statistical techniques analysing enormous datasets. The application of statistical models for machine-learning have exploded over the last decade due to availability of increased computing power and big data. In 2008, Chris Anderson, the editor-in-chief of the influential *Wired* magazine polemically stated: '*The End of Theory: the data deluge makes the scientific method obsolete.*' In his article, Anderson declared:

> At petabyte scale, information is not a matter of simple three- and four-dimensional taxonomy and order but of dimensionally agnostic statistics. . . .It forces us to view data mathematically first and establish a context for it later . . . Petabytes allow us to say: 'Correlation is enough'. (Anderson 2008)

The argument was summarily dismissed by critics and subjected to reproval (e.g. see boyd and Crawford 2012). It is not necessarily the case that the larger the volume and variety of data there is, more meaningful patterns can be discovered leading to greater accuracy of predictions and knowledge of the social world. Nevertheless, Anderson was prescient in identifying the trajectory of AI-big data analytics, predicated on the *fallacious* belief that 'data speaks for itself' (D'Ignazio and Klein 2020).

Machine learning uses a variety of formats of data, which can be based on 'supervised', 'unsupervised' and 'reinforcement' approaches.[8] Supervised learning models rely on labelled data to train a machine-learning model to make decisions. For instance, using a labelled set of images of breeds of dogs as training data. Input with a new image, the model classifies or predicts the label of the breed of dog. Supervised learning can also be used to predict outcomes, such as forecasting house prices. In contrast, unsupervised learning aims to *discover* patterns in data without knowing the outcomes in advance. These machine-learning models are trained with unstructured data. There are no labels identified to model relationships between inputs and outputs. Unsupervised learning is designed to organize the data and describe or represent its underlying structures (without knowing in advance which features are significant). It can be used to find customer segments in marketing data or in developing recommendation systems (e.g. as used by YouTube and Netflix to recommend what next to watch). Unlike supervised and unsupervised approaches, reinforcement learning has no training dataset, and 'learns' through trial and error or a mechanism of rewards and penalties. It develops an action model that seeks to maximize rewards via feedback from its environment. Reinforcement learning is used in real-time decision-making systems, and in fields such as robotics, driver-less vehicles and computer gaming. Additionally, Reinforcement Learning from Human Feedback (RLHF) is gaining popularity. It can be combined with unsupervised learning and incorporate human input. A RLHF can be trained more quickly, and be guided by humans to avoid errors or undesirable outputs.

Architectures of artificial neural networks, particularly 'deep learn-ing' (which may use supervised, unsupervised and reinforcement/RLHF learning), are receiving extraordinary research and development funding because of their supposed accuracy of classification and prediction.[9] These machine-learning models can detect relationships and patterns in potentially boundless amounts of data: 'nearly all pivot around ways of transform-ing, constructing or imposing some kind of shape on the data and using that shape to discover, decide, classify, rank, cluster, recommend, label or predict what is happening or what will happen' (MacKenzie 2015, 415). It is not easy to comprehensively understand how machine learning makes predictions without a working knowledge of computer algorithms and advanced statistics. Nonetheless, gaining an insight into how these predic-tive systems work helps to unravel the performative power of algorithms in rendering our contemporary world governable by the logics of machine reasoning (Pasquinelli 2017).

Mateo Pasquinelli succinctly describes machine-learning algorithms, such as neural networks, being designed to 'automate *statistical induction*'. They learn patterns in data to create a model that is able to predict future outcomes, which involves identifying relationships between input features and output values to be predicted. Features are the attributes or 'dimensions' of data. Earlier forms of machine-learning statistical analysis were limited by the number of variables and size of samples, and based on labelled data which was time consuming and costly to gather. To obviate the 'garbage in, garbage out' problem, selecting appropriate inputs (known as 'feature engineering') involved domain expertise of the datasets by machine-learning practitioners (McQuillan 2022). In contrast, contemporary forms of machine learning are less reliant on domain knowledge (or labelled data), because in the era of 'big data', almost anything can be reduced to a numerical value and be counted as a feature: texts, images, videos, sensor data, social media interactions, loca-tion, biometrics and so on (MacKenzie 2015). It is this inordinate potential capacity of machine learning, to 'inductively' work (e.g. 'unsupervised' model creation) in high-dimensional spaces – discovering correlations and patterns among multitudinous features – that enables hidden and complex relationships in data to be identified.

Deep learning models are designed to data-mine for association rules, dis-cover hidden patterns or subgroups, or to detect anomalies in messy, diverse or high-dimensional data by using algorithmic techniques such as clustering, visualization or dimensionality reduction. The term 'deep learning' refers to the depth of layers of *neural networks* used to analyse data. A neural net-work architecture – supposedly mimicking the organization of neurons of the human brain – consists of interconnected nodes, arranged in series of layers (see figure 2.2).

Input layer   Hidden layers   Output layer

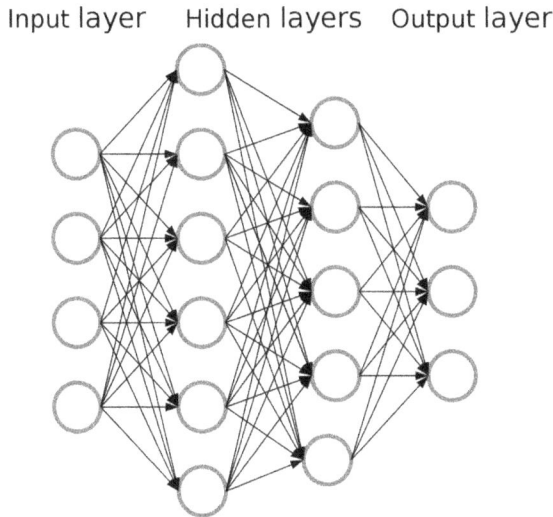

Figure 2.2   Neural Network Architecture.

Each layer processes inputs that feed outputs to an adjacent layer. Data signals transverse the network via nodes activating other nodes based on their 'weightings' and reaching threshold values. The training of neural networks commonly occurs through 'back propagation', which continuously 'tune' weightings and adjust thresholds for each iteration. Depending on the density of the neural network, the connections and dynamic weightings of the nodes through the layers can involve millions of calculations. Deep learning models have 'hidden' layers because the outputs between the layers, or how nodes are processing data as it propagates across the network is not accessible to human interpretation. McQuillan (2022) concludes that the neural 'network can't tell us why a particular pattern in any layer is significant: it delivers a prediction, not an explanation' (22).

Both supervised and unsupervised learning commonly use statistical techniques of regression which seek to find relationships between features that have the most impact. Advanced methods of regression train a deep learning model via *optimization* such as 'stochastic gradient descent' by assigning weights (optimal values) to features of the dataset. Gradient descent continually analyses and adjusts small random changes in weights and thresholds with different inputs. Optimization is a process that minimizes the loss function (the difference or error between actual and predicted values). These calculations are iteratively performed, possibly hundreds or thousands of times, until the direction of the gradient reaches its optimal value – the tuning process no longer reduces the error and the highest accuracy of the prediction model is presumably achieved.

Gradient descent is visualized as 'machine reasoning' operating in a landscape in which the goal is to reach the bottom of a 'valley', representing the minimized loss. However, methods of optimization are far from consummate or effortless processes. The development and training of deep learning models are based on numerous engineering decisions and interventions, the availability and assumptions about data, types of statistical techniques and modes of training. In practice, the predictive accuracy of these models is fundamentally questionable: 'the landscape rarely consists of a unique valley, and can be filled with various dips and crevices that will trap an unwary algorithm ... [T]his invisible complexity should cast doubt on any claim made by deep learning to produce a singular truth' (McQuillan 2022, 21). Furthermore, it is not only the imputed efficacy of machine-learning models based on the 'objectivity' of statistical methods that is problematic. McQuillan points to a type of *rationality* operating:

> a mode of calculative ordering that results in particular ways of structuring systems. The logic of optimization, which has deep Cold War roots, already underpins our systems of logistics and planning, and the combination of granular data and machine learning opens up the opportunity for it to be used for social problems (15).

The celebrated statistician, George P. Box (1976) famously stated that 'All models are wrong, but some are useful'. It is naive to suggest that software developers are unaware of how their models are approximations of reality. Yet the calculative rationality of deploying these models eschews treating them as mathematical abstractions. The *statistical* methods that machine-learning depends on measure, classify, correlate and predict. These models are wilfully deployed to make decisions and intervene in the world, constitutive of generating realities (cf. Hacking 1990; Amoore 2020). And as Pasquinelli (2017) elaborates: 'Within neural networks (as according also to the classical cybernetic framework), information becomes control; that is, a numerical input retrieved from the world turns into a control function of the same world' (2).

Pre-emption – In/Security

The control function (as discussed in part I) is tied to how post-raciality intersects with biopolitics – regulating degrees of normality of populations by managing the shifting boundaries between the normal and abnormal. In an *age of uncertainty* these boundaries are imploding. As Brian Massumi (2005) announced, 'Insecurity. . .is the new normal', in response to the 9/11 attacks in New York, USA. This momentous event transformed and fortified state surveillance and securitization, leading to a 'digital carceral infrastructure' (Wang 2018) in which data-driven *predictive* policing and counter-terrorism expanded and intensified, targeting racialized groups across the world. Although regimes of surveillance have not been 'inaugurated by new technologies' as Simone Browne in *Dark Matters* (2015) reminds us; rather 'to see it as ongoing is to insist that we factor in how racism and antiblackness undergird and sustain the intersecting surveillance of our present order' (8).

Western nation-states have failed to reckon with how neocolonial domination, neoliberal instabilities and racialized structural violence foment what is speciously labelled as 'crime', 'illegal immigration' or 'Islamic terrorism'. Contrary to addressing these issues as complex socioeconomic or geopolitical problems, there has been a turn to techno-solutionist ideologies to manage security, uncertainty and predicting risk:

> In the age of 'big data,' uncertainty is presented as an information problem that can be overcome with comprehensive data collection, statistical analysis that can identify patterns and relationships, and algorithms that can determine future outcomes. (Wang 2018, 238).

The rapid rise of predictive policing since the late 2000s has been built on opaque, propriety algorithmic models which claim to forecast where and when crime takes place. Not only are these systems designed to enhance efficiency and resource utilization for modern policing, they purport to mitigate human bias in law enforcement decision-making. The for-profit company, PredPol (renamed Geolitica) pioneered the adoption of crime prediction software applications. The software – inspired by earlier Pentagon military funding – was developed through a collaboration between researchers from the University of California and the LA Police Department. Algorithms used to predict earthquakes after-shocks were re-purposed to forecast the time and place of urban 'hot spots' supposedly at more risk, based on 'near-repeat' offences criminology theories (Shapiro 2017). The PredPol algorithmic model is trained on recorded crimes and estimates risk based on existing police data.

Critics of PredPol pointed to the fundamentally flawed nature of police data used to identify 'hot spots', because histories of institutionalized racism – and the colonial origins of policing racial others (Brogden 1987) – have entrenched the disproportionate targeting and over-policing of minoritized communities. Josh Scannell (2019) echoes the fact that predictive policing does not predict future crime; rather, it coordinates future policing by directing carceral state violence and power. Scannell draws on the work of Ruth Wilson Gilmore's characterization of the criminal justice system as organized through *racism*, critically defined as 'the state sanctioned or extralegal

production and exploitation of group-differentiated vulnerability to prema-
ture death' (Gilmore 2007, 247). Scannell continues by stating, 'the inverted
world of predictive policing, group-differentiated vulnerability is translated
into probable criminal "risk." Predictive policing software uses almost every
conceivable measure of vulnerability and victimization' (2019, 111).

The burgeoning critiques of predictive policing have not curtailed the
advancement of so-called AI applications, venturing to move beyond the possible historical biases of police data. HunchLab, developed by the geospatial
technology company Azavea, innovated a big data analytics approach. It
infers greater accuracy for predicting crime, by expanding and diversifying
data sources and *measures*, including infrastructural and environmental characteristics of areas, which can include temporal patterns (seasonality), risk
terrain modelling (locations of amenities), socioeconomic indicators. Azavea
(2014) claim that their system

> automatically learns what is important for each crime type and provides recom-
> mendations of where to focus the resources that you have available. If you don't
> have particular datasets (such as bars or bus stops), the system simply adapts to
> use the data available in a given jurisdiction (10).

HunchLab was sold to ShotSpotter in 2019, who renamed it as 'Community First Patrol Management Software'. ShotSpotter on their website state
their big data predictive software is 'Mitigating Bias' by using 'Objective,
Non-Crime Data'. They promote dynamic AI modelling which purportedly
produces scientifically unbiased crime forecasting.

Companies developing contemporary predictive police software maintain
their products are *race-neutral* because no explicit data of the 'protected'
ethno-racial characteristics of individuals are collected in modelling crime.
Critics have foregrounded how algorithmic statistical correlations (unintentionally) produce disparate impacts that disproportionately harm people
of colour (O'Neil 2016). For example, 'variables' such as neighbourhood
boundaries, types of shops, educational achievement or loan repayment when
correlated can operate as *discriminatory proxies* of race – leading to amplifying *risk* estimates of crime in racialized and impoverished areas. Predictive
policing is an exemplary *post-racial* practice, as it does not need to rely on the
category of race to be racist (cf. Bonilla Silva 2006). Notably, Chun (2021)
reminds us that when proxies are 'used to seek the unknown or absent, they
introduce uncertainty, even as they serve to reduce it. Proxies are necessary
and inadequate: indeed, they point to inadequacies in direct knowledge more
generally' (136). The measures of proxies are fundamental to how uncertainty exists in data-driven decision-making systems.

The companies behind the development of predictive policing technologies
claim greater accuracy in determining the risk of crime, in comparison to

prejudiced human decision-making. In reality, it is practically impossible to evaluate the efficacy of crime forecasting systems. A key goal of predictive policing has been the *prevention* of crime. In this regard, the 'performativity of prediction' (MacKenzie 2015) intervenes in the space it inhabits – the success of preventing crime is not easily discernible.

> The result is an indeterminacy that is fundamental to prediction in general . . . but which has largely been unacknowledged in debates about big data policing . . . Predictive efficacy is essentially an estimation of deterrence, which is unobservable. (Shapiro 2019, 463)

The fact there is no substantive evidence of predictive policing decreasing crime has led to these technologies being circuitously defended on 'the grounds that "the results . . . are probabilistic, not certain"' (RAND Corporation, cited in Scannell 2019, 111).

The *indeterminacy* of prediction haunts the pursuit of state securitization, and is acutely manifested in practices of counter-terrorism. Acts of terrorism are experienced as high impact, devastating events which can lead to profound social changes (Taleb 2007). Yet contrary to the production of everyday fears in the Global North, terrorism *rarely* happens. Accurately predicting terrorism is nearly impossible because it does not follow stable patterns of occurrence and remains a low-frequency, improbable event (Huey et al. 2015). Moreover, there is a wide consensus among security researchers that identifying 'terrorists' via algorithmic-based mass surveillance is extraordinarily challenging due to the 'base rate fallacy'. There are only likely to be a few actual terrorists in a population: 'it's a very difficult job to identify suspects, just from slightly abnormal patterns in the normal things that everybody does' (Goldacre 2009). In practice, as Munk chillingly deduces, it can lead to identifying '100,000 false positives for every real terrorist'. Nevertheless, the inability of intelligence agencies to predict the 9/11 terror attacks was presented in terms of a calamitous failure of securitization when confronted with an *inscrutable* Islamic threat to (white) Western civilization.

The War on Terror (WoT) shifted the grounds on which calculating risk and the logics post-racial biopolitical control operate. The 'performativity of prediction' progressed from *prevention* managing determinate threats in a knowable world, to *pre-emption* facing perpetual, indeterminate threats in an unknowable, uncontrollable world (Massumi 2015). According to Massumi, pre-emption marks an epochal reconfiguration in the ecology of power and control, which exists in conditions of the 'indeterminate potentiality' of protean threats: 'an ever-presence of indiscriminate threat, riddled with the anywhere-anytime potential for the *proliferation of the abnormal*' (Massumi

2015, 26; my emphasis). He notes that the 'enemy' may be expected to be from an ethnic (Arab) or religious (Muslim) group, but the possibility exists that they could also be a 'white Briton'.

The near impossibility of accurately identifying terrorists or auguring acts of terrorism has not led to security agencies abandoning algorithmic predictive models. On the contrary, pre-emption has intensified the reliance on surveillant big data analytics. There has been change in what Amoore (2013) identifies as the *calculus of risk* of pre-emption:

> It seeks not to forestall the future via calculation but to incorporate the very unknowability and profound uncertainty of the future into imminent decision ... To manage risks ahead of time is to enroll modes of calculation that can live with emergence itself, embrace and reincorporate the capacity for error, false positive, mistake, and anomaly (9).

Both Massumi and Amoore highlight pre-emption as both responding to and precipitating indeterminacy, insecurity and crises. What I want to foreground is how the performativity of pre-emption is insidiously *race-making* (cf. Vukov 2016). It prevails in *post-racial* conditions of the unfathomable threat of an unknowable other – the '*proliferation of the abnormal*'.[10] Recall how the post-racial is animated by the biopolitical regulation of the norm as 'an interplay of differential normalities' (Foucault 2007, 63). Post-racial pre-emption is indifferent to the binary division of the normal/abnormal. The distinction between low-/high-risk populations, or safe/risky subjects (the 'suspect' or 'person of interest'), is not exigently a stable or invariable category in counter-terrorism discourse (Kafer 2019).

The racial profiling of populations, especially those identified as 'Muslims', by counter-terrorism practices have been rightly condemned. Although what can be overlooked is how shifts from prevention to pre-emption are buttressed by the possibility of state security machine-learning predictive algorithms eschewing relying on pre-existing ethno-racial characteristics. In reality, we know that such characteristics are indeterminate: 'not all Middle Eastern Muslims are terrorists, and not all terrorists are from the Middle East' (Munk 2017).

The post-racial condition marks the mutability of race as *informational*, resulting in the 'Muslim Terrorist' emerging as a 'statistical population', as Jasbir Puar elaborates:

> In statistical terms, race and sex are experienced as a series of transactional informational flows captured . . . and render bodies transparent or opaque, secure or insecure, risky or at risk, risk-enabled or risk-disabled, the living or the living dead. Terrorist bodies as a 'statistical population' . . . perversely

transcends national boundaries . . . uncontainable, spontaneous, and untraceable. (2007, 160)

A key innovation of contemporary machine learning (e.g. deep learning) is the ability to fashion algorithmic models beyond the limited dimensionality of known variables such age, gender or ethnicity. These models 'learn' by being exposed to the expansive volume and variety of 'big data' (features) such as social media posts and interactions, reading habits, search history, contact lists and networked associations, financial transactions, phone calls, location and travel destinations, country of origin, signifiers of religiosity, biometrics, etc. Features can potentially include boundless types of data attributes existing in a space of high multi-dimensionality (Munk 2017; Amoore 2021).

Amoore challenges the attested computational efficacy and objectivity of machine-learning models exposed to big data, operating in high-dimensional feature space. In particular, she confronts the deployment of deep learning algorithms for immigration and border security; and echoes Scannell when highlighting the 'political space' of racialized group-differentiated violence these decision-making systems are constituting:

the feature space is a political space that is positively enhanced by its exposure to volatility and social instability . . . and therefore can both withstand and profit from the societal fractures or geopolitical violence it is exposed to. (Amoore 2021, 4)

More specifically, these algorithmic systems function as 'racializing assemblages' involved in the differentiation and hierarchization of populations in the biopolitical management of the abnormal (Weheliye 2014).

When characterizing machine-learning algorithms as racializing assemblages, we can consider how they depend on methods of statistical analysis. The field of statistics was historically developed to 'objectively' address real-world questions and problems of variation and uncertainty, particularly for characterizing and delineating populations (Hacking 1990). The celebrated narratives of statistics revolutionizing knowledge and understanding in the natural sciences belie how these advances were not outside of prevailing racial-colonial ideologies of 'white prototypicality' – the ideal norm or standard that orders life (Amaro 2019a). Pioneers of statistics such as Francis Galton, Adolphe Quetlet and Karl Pearson created influential concepts of correlation, probability and regression, which were deeply entangled with abhorrent projects of eugenics and racial science (Clayton 2021). Pearson, for example, pioneered statistical correlation to develop eugenics that could be subjected to predictive control (Chun 2021; Hong 2022).

Drawing on the critique of Western humanism and eugenic/dysgenic selection by Sylvia Wynter, Ramon Amaro (2019b) observes that the 'conditions for racial sorting and priority were already set forth in the establishment of data analytics and statistical correlation as viable tools for social inquiry'. This is not to facilely claim that algorithms, or the statistical methods that underpin them, are indelibly racist. Rather, it is to understand predictive machine learning systems in relation to the 'underlying principles of mathematics as the engine that drives data towards languages of normality and truth prior to any operational discomforts or violences' (2019b).

The common assumption that algorithms are technically neutral and being exposed to biased or 'bad' data may corrupt their outputs fails to reckon with their normalizing mathematical architectures. Pre-emptive algorithmic systems are not merely transformed by bad data into conduits propagating discrimination. The calculus of risk in the algorithmic identification of an 'illegal immigrant' or 'suspect terrorist' operates on, as Gary Kafer argues,

> logics of racialization that are encoded into specific computational parameters. Algorithms do not become racialised when encountering data imbued with elements of sociopolitical difference, but rather *mobilise logics of racialisation in order to process data assemblages.* (2019, 31)

The outputs of pre-emptive, machine-learning algorithms of securitization are based on statistical estimates of riskiness, which may be constantly varying. These systems are conditioned by the post-racial mutability of race. That is, an algorithmic onto-epistemology modulating the normal vs. abnormal (the safe vs. risky subject) in the production of a norm. From a materialist standpoint, we can avoid reducing these shifting grounds as arising uniquely from changing probability calculations, and instead highlight they are structured by a post-racial force of biopolitical normalization 'producing and rearranging racial difference' (Saldanha 2007, 197). This is more than considering race as a 'floating signifier' (Hall 1997) which shows how arbitrary human and non-human differences are *represented* in relation to changing sociopolitical conditions.

Algorithmic assemblages of securitization are generative – doing more than signifying, representing or profiling ethno-racial categories – they are *race-making*. As racializing assemblages, they inscribe forces of power and differentiation on to datafied bodies (cf. Weheliye 2014; Vukov 2016). The disparate attributes of suspect populations are *charged* by race, exceeding their forms of representation. These assemblages mobilize logics of racialization, which are *creating* 'racial formations, racial clusters. These clusters emerge immanently . . . Racial formations comprise multiple spatial scales and continually change over time' (Saldanha 2007, 190). To put it another way, the illegal immigrant or terrorist suspect is in an incessant and mutable state of post-racial algorithmic *emergence*. When discussing algorithms for securitization, Amoore (2021) maintains that algorithmically generated clusters or groups are 'deeply racialized all the way down' (6). It is this *race-making* capacity of algorithms that is difficult to grasp and analyse, yet is at the heart of digital technologies of post-racial control.

Part II began with the example of the Ofqual algorithm producing discriminatory educational results for racialized and vulnerable populations. While the focus shifted to examining more complex AI/machine-learning algorithms, the fundamental problem remains that decision-making systems are entrenching existing inequities and generating new kinds. While there is increasing attention being paid to the social harms caused by algorithms, it has been argued that we need to move beyond notions of bias, and instead focus on social control. By considering algorithms as post-racial assemblages, we uncover their essential role in upholding a techno-social order that conceals its own authority.

There are concerns that critiques of these algorithmic systems are being side-lined by the clamour to develop human-like 'Artificial General Intelligence' (AGI). The accompanying dystopia that AGI will become 'self-aware' and surpass humanity is arguably symptomatic of a crisis of authority and whiteness (Ali 2019), when technology no longer functions as an agency of social control and instead becomes 'out of control'.

The deployment of automated systems is not dangerous on the dystopian grounds that a future form of AGI will overtake the world. Rather, the danger is that contemporary algorithmic systems are *already* in place, making decisions over our lives and impacting on the marginalized and most vulnerable populations (Noble 2018; Benjamin 2019). The efforts of regulatory controls thus far have been wholly inadequate in curtailing the deployment of discriminatory algorithmic decision-making in welfare, education, finance, criminal justice, surveillance and border controls. The technical 'values' embodied in the design features of algorithms based on performance, efficiency and optimization need to be challenged as antithetical to building societies that support the most vulnerable.

NOTES

1. The Ofqual statistical model is an example of a form of 'rule-based' algorithm, which essentially relies on hard-coded rules and inferences to process data and make decisions. In contrast, 'machine-learning' algorithms make decisions based on 'learning' from the data (e.g. looking for correlations). Machine-learning algorithms are effectively opaque by design. Although in reality, the complexity of rule-based algorithms can be similarly difficult to ascertain, as discovered in the case of the Ofqual algorithm.

2. For example, if the algorithm predicted three fail grades for a subject, then the three lowest rated students would receive this grade irrespective of what teachers may have predicted (Haines 2020).

3. John McCarthy (2007) offers the following definition of AI: 'It is the science and engineering of making intelligent machines, especially intelligent computer programs. It is related to the similar task of using computers to understand human intelligence, but AI does not have to confine itself to methods that are biologically observable' (2). Machine learning is a subset or application of AI, which enables computers to learn without being explicitly pre-programmed. The question of what constitutes computer 'intelligence' is highly contentious.

4. 'Tone policing' refers to silencing or derailing a discussion by criticizing a person's emotion rather than content.

5. Machine-learning training come in different forms, including 'supervised', 'unsupervised' or 'reinforcement' learning (and based on different formats of labelled and unlabeled training data). This will be discussed later.

6. Suresh and Guttag acknowledge there are different methods of identifying harm, for example see Ntoutsi et al. (2020) and Mehrabi et al. (2021). Stokes refers to an earlier version of the machine-learning life-cycle diagram, which was posted by Deborah Raji (a computer science activist and researcher) on the Gebru-LeCun Twitter thread. Although Stokes does not make the effort to discover that the diagram originates from a medium post by Suresh, which was updated in the final paper published by Suresh and Guttag (2021).

7. Stokes also exploits the post-racial *'debatability'* over how racism is deflected and denied (cf. Titley 2019), which is further discussed in part III.

8. While these machine-learning approaches are distinct, in actual applications, a combination of different approaches can be used. For example, HunchLab uses both supervised and unsupervised learning; and algorithmic recommendation systems may use a hybrid approach.

9. Currently, these models depend on analysing large datasets, involving significant computing power which consume enormous amounts of energy. This field is revered as the 'holy grail' of machine learning, based on developing unsupervised and reinforcement deep learning models trained with relatively little data, to be applied to any task.

10. Pre-emptive algorithms of securitization are arguably structured by a form of racial paranoia. The algorithmic *compulsion* is to find (meaningful) correlations or patterns in big data to discover unknowable Islamic terrorists or pre-empt unpredictable acts of terrorism (see Sharma and Nijjar 2018).

Part III

Scale

The internet has transformed from a gamut of hyper-linked web pages into a never-ending digital media 'stream'. Alexis Madrigal (2013) for *The Atlantic* magazine, portrays the stream by its speed, immediacy and real-timeness when he writes: 'The Stream represents the triumph of reverse-chronology, where importance – above-the-foldness – is based exclusively on nowness.' It is replete with viral events of breaking news or political revolts, as well as the frenetic circulation of celebrity gossip, banal chatter, images, videos and irreverent memes. Social media platforms such as YouTube, TikTok, Facebook, Instagram, Twitter and Reddit are key players in generating the stream. These platforms seek to algorithmically 'curate' the stream while insatiably monetizing the enormous amounts of user-generated content.

Alongside Madrigal, social media commentators writing a decade ago characterized the stream as creating 'a different form of syndication which cannot be licensed and cannot be controlled' (Schonfeld 2009), one that 'has reached peak hate' (Marche 2013). The stream has been depicted as undermining the editorial authority of traditional media gate-keepers, fitfully usurping the control of governments, and unleashing online 'hate'. The challenge of regulating the stream offers the potential for creating alternative spaces of online interaction, enabling marginalized voices to be heard. The cultural critic, Sydette Harry remarked: 'The stream that disquiets Madrigal is really a flood, and it has burst open the gates of established media, bringing with it things that do not fit so neatly in that locked box' (2014). However, Madrigal's lament of the loss of control over online information became the dominant framing over the last decade. In 2021 the UN Secretary-General António Guterres upheld that 'social media provides a global megaphone for hate'. Online communication is depicted as transgressing societal norms – the propagation of insults, abuse and threats have become increasingly common

51

experiences, especially for marginalized groups. Acknowledging the wide-spread problem of online hate has been welcomed by civil and human rights organizations (Amnesty International 2018; Hope not hate 2022).

Discussions exploring different kinds of mediated online hostility prolifer-ate terms such as flaming, griefing, trolling, harassment, abuse, doxing and cyber-bullying. 'Hate' has become the moniker collectively describing the multitude of these different types of antagonism (Sheperd et al. 2015). Yet characterizing social media as a raging stream filled with hate has done little to advance a critical understanding of what are *particular* forms of online antagonism and why they occur. What is common to this discourse is present-ing social media as a debased environment circulating *hate* which is difficult to thwart.

The causes and forms of 'online hate' are manifold. No wonder media commentators and researchers flit between a range of explanations: blaming users or organized far-right groups, the effects of online disinhibition, the design of social media platforms virally circulating information, recommen-dation algorithms promoting sensationalist content, and inadequate modera-tion practices. A key cause for concern has been the increasing dominance of Big Tech social media platforms determining networked communications. In particular, the 'infrastructuralization of platforms' (Poell et al. 2019) highlights how corporate digital platforms are embedded in the social and technical infrastructures of society, leading to centralization of power, a lack of civic accountability, and the rise of surveillant capitalism.[1]

Witney Phillips (2018), writing a decade after Madrigal, shifts our attention to the functioning of Big Tech. The metaphor of the uncontrollable flow of the stream is transformed into a full-blown crisis of the *toxicity* of networked communications: 'The media landscape is overrun with toxic narratives and polluted information not because our systems are broken, but because our systems are working.' The hyper-connectivity of social media has created a participatory medium that foments communicative-overload, dis-informa-tion, manipulation and 'hate', spurred by a corporate 'attention-economy'. Platform-engineered practices of info-virality are imploding boundaries of truth versus falsity, eroding the integrity of democratic deliberation, and pre-cipitating the spread of online hate (Phillips and Milner 2021).

Greater governmental and corporate attention is being paid to tackling the toxic environment of social media, involving banning malicious user accounts, fact-checking to curtail dis-information, and regulating platforms to expunge 'hate speech'. These current, mainly techno-solutionist efforts, remain lim-ited and inconsistent. There is no technical 'fix' or a singular solution to what are complex and variegated historically determined problems, compounded and amplified by digital media. The existence of dis-information and 'hate' precede the internet, and their entanglement with digital technologies has made these issues more difficult to address. While a burgeoning academic literature is exploring forms of online dis-information and hate, there has been a relative lack of research theorizing social media racism.[2] I offer an account of online media racism analysing the co-constitutive relationship between the social and digital. Stating the intention to conduct a *sociotechnical* analysis has become commonplace, though it remains challenging to unpack how racism and the online are entangled.

It will be argued that notions of 'hate' are too nebulous and counterproductive to develop an approach able to capture the specific dynamics of techno-racism. Online racism is difficult to grasp due to its multifarious formations and manifestations. I contend that post-raciality renders racism as either an 'exceptional' phenomenon (an extreme social aberration) or, conversely, a 'natural' human condition (anyone can be racist). While operating from seemingly incongruous standpoints, both jettison a critical account of racism, emptying out its histories and politics.

At the risk of caricature, sociological and technology-based thinking about online racism has operated in their disciplinary silos, methodologically overlooking the (post-racial) mutability of contemporary racism from a sociotechnical standpoint. Sociological accounts have presented racism as a 'real' world phenomenon that spills over into the 'virtual', accelerated and amplified by digital technologies. In comparison, technology-based accounts see online racism as a prosaic phenomenon principally caused by the affordances of communicative technologies. Both accounts diverge in their explanation of online racism, yet they are equally reductive in its conception. The former valorizes racism as a socially determined phenomenon by ignoring its 'emergent' formations, vis-à-vis digital technologies, while the latter is technologically determinist because of its historically devoid grasp of racial formations.

I develop a framework to understand the protean forms and flows of social media racism. Alongside other types of online antagonism, such as misogyny and homophobia, racism occurs across different digital platforms, with varying frequency, magnitude, intensity and affect. Its communicative mode may take the form of a text, image, GIF, video or meme, appearing as a post, comment, (re)tweet, hashtag or 'like', etc. Online racism can be a sustained attack on a person of colour, or target a whole minoritized group or organization they belong too. It can be propagated by individual users, spontaneous or organized networked crowds, or via bots and algorithms. The forms of (post-)racial expression can morph as it traverses the web, gaining traction and visibility across different platforms, while resisting interpretation and condemnation (see part I).

To grasp the multi-modality of social media racism, the notion of assemblages can be extended in relation to *scale*.[3] The 'flat ontology' of assemblages (DeLanda 2013) can engage with how the agency of human actors, digital technologies and forms of racism are entangled and emergent on social media platforms. By conjoining assemblage thinking with the concept of scale, we can begin to fathom the multiplicity of online racism. Scale is conceived as more than size, or the conventional distinction between the macro and micro. Social entities and phenomena can exist and operate at disparate levels, and emerge through networked interactions across multiple scales (Horton 2021).

The account of scale underpins an approach that grapples with the differential forms, registers, (in)visibilities, levels and temporalities of racism manifested online as a 'complex system'. Two relational scales will be identified concerning what I call *spectacular* and *ambient* modes of online racism. These are figuratively derived from a 'power law' distribution which can describe the skewed and capricious characteristics of networked phenomena. The magnitude, intensity and affects of racism can be analysed through a multi-scalar lens. My aim is to offer a framework that takes seriously the medium as generative in proliferating online racism while avoiding bifurcating the social and the technological.

THE PROBLEM WITH HATE

> Although it is hard to find research that has statistics measuring the volume of hate speech online, it does appear to be increasing dramatically. This might reflect a change in the way we communicate rather than an increase in the amount of hateful speech taking place. (Bartlett et al. 2014, 11).

The *Anti-Social Media* report produced by the think-tank Demos contends that there are increasing amounts of hate speech online.[4] Importantly, Bartlett et al. speculate whether it has been accelerated by the ease of online communications or worsening societal conditions escalating expressions of online hate. Further, they point out that patterns of hate speech are complex, and that the term lacks a single meaning. The notion of 'hate' identifies a breadth of harmful actions and behaviours directed at a range of groups of people. The scope of the term is remarkably broad.

The UN Strategy and Plan of Action on Hate Speech (UN 2019) acknowledges that while there is no international legal definition of hate speech, it can be understood as

> any kind of communication in speech, writing or behaviour, that attacks or uses pejorative or discriminatory language with reference to a person or a group on the basis of who they are, in other words, based on their religion, ethnicity, nationality, race, colour, descent, gender or other identity factor.

The UN document goes on to identify the impact on hate speech in relation to the limits of 'free speech', human rights protection, countering terrorism and extremism, gender-based violence, protecting refugees and fighting 'against all forms of racism and discrimination'. In recognition of the problem of hate, there has been considerable growth of academic research and increasing public concern (Paz et al. 2020). Studying the escalation of hate online reached the genre of 'popular science' books, exemplified by the publication of *The Science of Hate: How Prejudice Becomes Hate and What We Can Do to Stop it*, by the researcher Matthew Williams (2022).

However, much of what is discussed as hate continues to be defined so broadly that it is in danger of collapsing and obfuscating the analyses of what are specific types of social antagonisms. In a discussion of the 'histories of hate', Tamara Sheperd et al. (2015) point to the struggle over 'what to call online hate. How do different labels for hate speech online implicate different modes of affect, violence, and social exclusion?' (3). And they stress that different terms such as 'a hater' or cyber-bullying, trolling and harassment 'represent different phenomena, behaviours, and underlying motivations . . . [T]hey have different definitions and are largely carried out by different groups of people' (4). For instance, racism can be driven by organized far-right groups on the notorious imageboard 8kun (8chan), or by ordinary users circulating memes on TikTok; or in the form of sub-tweets on Twitter, or vitriolic comments on YouTube (Murthy and Sharma 2019). Comparably, Debbie Ging and Eugenia Siapera (2018), from a feminist digital media perspective, maintain that the concept of hate (speech) is too limiting to sufficiently assay the discursive modalities and causes of online misogyny.

A fundamental concern remains with conceptions of hate rooted in understanding social antagonisms from a behaviourist logic of *prejudice* (Bonilla-Silva 2015). This has especially been a problem with sociology and psychology perspectives reductively conceiving racism (on- or off-line) as the flawed beliefs and attitudes of misguided individuals, rather than analysing racism as a systemic, historically determined phenomena (Daniels 2013). In accounts of prejudice, racism is ahistorically presented in terms of the intentionality or pathology of actors; whether they are die-hard racists or ordinary users making inflammatory comments due to the effects of online disinhibition.

Hate framed through the logic of 'racism-as-prejudice' has led to two mainstream explanations of online racism, operating at different levels. These can be labelled as *extreme ('macro') racism* which is considered exceptional to societal norms; and *ordinary ('micro') racism* arising vis-à-vis daily online interactions (cf. Lentin 2016; Siapera 2019). Extreme racism is manifested by the grievous targeting of minority groups via threats of violence or abhorrent epithets. Its visibility and impact can be significant. In contrast, while ordinary racism is offensive, its expressions can appear less threatening in the form of demotic name-calling, slurs and 'micro-aggressions' (cf. Sue 2010). In reality, the articulation of these kinds of racism is not always simple to distinguish. Take, for example, the impact of the ignominious 4Chan /b board on wider internet and meme culture, which can take the form of an ideologically-driven racist mimicking being a playful troll, or an ordinary user (unwittingly) propagating coded racialized memes which were originally spawned on 4Chan. Regardless of intentionality, these practices propagate either or both forms of extreme and ordinary racism in the pursuit of 'the lulz' (Phillips and Milner 2017).

It is useful to explore the supposed characteristics of extreme and ordinary racism because it highlights the challenge of developing a critical account of online racism, outside of the limits of the discourse of hate. Notably, what counts as 'unacceptable hate speech' largely focuses on forms of extreme racism and struggles to address ordinary racist expression (Siapera 2019). From a perspective that insists racism has been integral to the formation of Western societies, Goldberg (1997) points out that racist expressions are more than 'hate', and their articulations are not only extreme or exceptional:

> Racist expressions however, are various in kind – in disposition, in emotive effect, in intention, and in outcome . . . Racist expressions are normal . . . manifest not only in extreme epithets but in insinuations and suggestions, in reasoning and representation, in short, in microexpressions of daily life. Racism is not – or more exactly is not simply or only – about hate (20).

Neoliberal societies, via shifting human rights discourses and anti-discrimination legislation, have given recognition to 'hate speech'. It has become a central tenet for making visible *extreme racism*, rooted in (neo-)Nazi or far-right ideas and expression. The aggrandizement of term 'hate speech' is symptomatic of the post-racial in which racism is presented as an aberration, hoisted from the 'outside': 'racism symbolised . . . [by] the Nazis became in the Western imaginary the template for the racial "state of exception" . . . defined as extremist politics' (Sayyid and Hesse 2006, 29). The rendering of racist expression as an *exceptional* event of hate (speech) is divorced from grasping how racism pervades social relations. Alana Lentin (2005) reminds us, 'far from being external to capitalist liberal-democratic nation-state, modern racism was a consequence of modernity' (2005, 381).

Ordinary racism, in contrast to its extreme 'macro' forms, is characterized as a seemingly common or even mundane 'micro' phenomenon, encountered or perpetuated by almost anyone who interacts on mainstream social media platforms.[5] Mainstream platforms such as Facebook, Twitter, YouTube, TikTok and Reddit are frequently singled out as sites brimming with abusive content, due to their poorly designed or lax moderation practices against hate speech (York and McSherry 2019). Rather than instigated by pathological actors (the 'real' extreme racists on odious sub-Reddits, far-right Gab, Parlor or chan sites), ordinary racism can supposedly involve any of us. Engagement in racialized expression and comment culture is considered to be primarily due to the *medium* itself, determined by the affordances of social media platforms.

Lisa Nakamura, in her perceptive essay 'Glitch Racism: Networks as Actors within Vernacular Internet Theory' (2013), interrogates 'ordinary', or what is labelled 'everyday' racism. She highlights that a populist explanation of online racism (and sexism) is exalted in the 'Greater Internet Fuckwad Theory' (GIFT): anonymity, depersonalization and 'imagined audiences' produce degenerate conditions coupled with platformed hyper-connectivity, for the unleashing of latent racist sentiments among ordinary users.[6] This account 'makes us all out to be the fuckwads. Identifying racist behaviour on the Internet as emanating from "normal people" foregrounds the act's technicity. It's not the actor, it's the network' (Nakamura 2013). The GIFT effaces the significance of racism, by declaring that anyone can hate, and it merely requires apposite conditions for expressions of online racism to surface.

Nakamura contends that the technological determinism of the GIFT hyperbolizing the affordances of the web, is common to understanding online racism both inside and outside of academia:

> It makes it clear that everyday racism is an effect of digital networks – the more pervasive and integrated into everyday life these networks become, and the more pseudonymity is available, the more racism that equation will produce, regardless of the intentions, feelings, or opinions of users. (Nakamura 2013)

It is interesting to observe that while the accounts of ordinary and extreme racism appear to differ in their assumptions and explanations, they share a reductive framing of hate. *Ordinary* racism as a contingent effect of the network is made banal because as Nakamura maintains, it is conceived as a 'glitch' (similar to noise or spam) in the network. In comparison, *extreme* racism is presented as an aberration to democratic societies (Lentin 2016). In both accounts, whether racism is made mundane or exceptional, the logic of 'hate-prejudice' forsakes acknowledging that racism is in fact 'anchored in material structures and embedded in historical configurations of power' (Stam and Shohat 1995, 19).

The discourse of hate fails to contend with the historically and politically contingent and shifting nature of racism. This has resulted in strategies countering hate being unable to address the contemporary protean forms and wild proliferations of online racism. I have described this phenomenon as a racialized info-overload, whereby 'casual racial banter, race-hate comments, griefing, images, videos and anti-racist sentiment bewilderingly intermingle, mash-up and virally circulate' (Sharma 2013, 47). Gavan Titley, in his book, *Racism and Media*, develops this discussion by highlighting the post-racial constestability and debatability over racism. He writes how racism is presented as

> simultaneously everywhere and nowhere . . . [T]he mention of racism as an invitation to refute its relevance. In the contemporary political context, to speak publicly about racism is to be immediately integrated into an intensive process of delineation, deflection and denial, a contest over who gets to define racism, when 'everyone' gets to speak about it. (2020, 2)

The notion of hate fails to address how discourses of racism have become deeply fractious. The limitations of hate are also revealed in assumptions about strategies to counter online hate. Legislation against hate speech and making social media companies responsible for content on their platforms are the primary means of eradicating racism in the anti-discrimination discourse addressing *extreme* racism. Concurrently, social media policies and moderation practices largely fail to curtail *ordinary* racism (Siapera 2019). Thus far, the efficacy of these counter hate strategies is questionable. By disregarding how racism appears 'everywhere and nowhere', mainstream interventions struggle to meaningfully identify hate and implement effective counter strategies. Furthermore, current practices can repress or deflect online racism, only for it to mutate and reappear in other forms and spaces (cf. Hughey and Daniels 2013). Counter hate strategies have been unable to grapple with the mutability and obfuscatory nature of contemporary racism, and sets apart an analysis of online communications from the 'real' world.

SCALING RACISM – POWER LAWS

I have argued that 'hate' has become the common-sense *post-racial* frame through which social media racism has been made (un)intelligible. Its limitations are manifold because of a problematic conception of racism and technological determinist account of mediated communication. This section develops an alternative sociotechnical framework based on a notion of *scale* to make sense of the complexity of online racism.

Social media racism resists any simple analysis because it operates on different 'scales' (more than the macro and micro), and affective registers. Racism on the web is a networked phenomenon, circulating and traversing many kinds of social media platforms. Its spacio-temporalities, magnitude, intensities and affects are volatile and multitudinous. Its extreme-macro and ordinary-micro forms are, in reality, recondite and mutable. Nor is it easy to distinguish between differing actors or agencies involved in propagating racism; whether un/intentionally by users, or via the online cultures of memes and trolling, or due to the technological affordances and architectures of platformed hyper-connectivity.

To begin to address the multi-modality of social media racism, we can consider the concept of scale alongside assemblages. One of the most insightful expositions is by Zachary Horton (2021):

> scale is a primary form of difference . . . in the sense that it is present on the scene and does its work before stable identities (subjects or objects) have formed along its spectrum . . . While often conflated with size, scale has many facets . . . It names a set of relations: external relations between two or more milieus, and internal relations between entities within a single milieu (4).

Horton's account of scale does not maintain sharp analytical distinctions between different phenomena, such as structure and agency, or the macro and micro. It shares similarities with the concept of assemblages (both are associated with materialist ontologies of emergence). Manuel DeLanda (2016) discusses assemblages as composed of heterogeneous components which are not solely defined in terms of size or level. What he means by the 'flat' (not horizontal) ontology of assemblages is that at any scale, the 'whole' can be analysed through the interactions of its parts. That is, 'entities operating at different scales can directly interact with one another (19), and assemblages 'merge from the interactions between their parts' (21).[7] Regarding assemblages through the lens of scale enables dynamic multi-scalar characteristics of phenomena or social entities to be highlighted. The emphasis is on differential relations and *emergent* events which can result in identifying systemic (macro) hierarchical orderings as well fleeting (micro) occurrences.

Simply put, while online racism appears volatile and inexorable, I utilize the idea of a multi-scalar lens to explore its emergence and propagation. As Horton (2021) suggests, we can consider scale imparting 'both a politics and an environment' (5). Though this begs the question, how can we make sense of multi-scalar, divergent modalities of online racism? My approach is to turn to a particular type of *power law distribution* ('long tail') to map the multi-scalar characteristics of the digitally mediated, networked spaces racism operates in.

Studies of digital networks over the last two decades mapped their *organizing* principles and structures (Barabasi and Bonabeau 2003). Earlier accounts of networks assumed randomness. In the case of the web, information was expected to be accessible and equally visible. As a measure of 'popularity' of web pages, most would have approximately the same number of incoming links from other web pages. Popularity would follow a 'normal distribution', with almost no web pages having either extremely large or small numbers of in-links. It was assumed that unique users with their diversity of interests generate patterns of connections to information that is fairly randomly distributed.

When researchers conducted empirical studies of the web, an entirely different kind of distribution was discovered: the popularity of web pages is highly skewed. In relative terms, a minority of web pages have huge numbers of in-links while the majority of pages have few in-links. This distribution of popularity follows a particular kind of 'power law'. The shape of this power law is often characterized by a steeply declining curve representing a system of ranking (Shirky 2003). It results in a highly unequal, skewed distribution often characterized by a 'head' at the uppermost part of the distribution, followed by a 'long tail' (see figure 3.1).

In comparison to the 'bell curve' of a normal distribution, when following a long tail power law, there will be more numbers of web pages that are extremely popular (at the head of the distribution), and significantly many more numbers of web pages that have little or almost no popularity (residing in the long tail). A fundamental feature of this type of power law distribution is that phenomena at the head of the tail are relatively rare in comparison to the long tail, though embody and express a concentration of power (Herod 2011). For example, there is a relatively small proportion of 'influential' Twitter users with millions of followers compared to the majority of Twitter users with, at most, a few hundred followers.

In addition to characterizing the internet, web and social media platforms, power law distributions can describe many other human and non-human phenomena, such as the size of colonies of bacteria, the magnitude of earthquakes, the spread of infectious diseases, causalities in war, word frequencies,

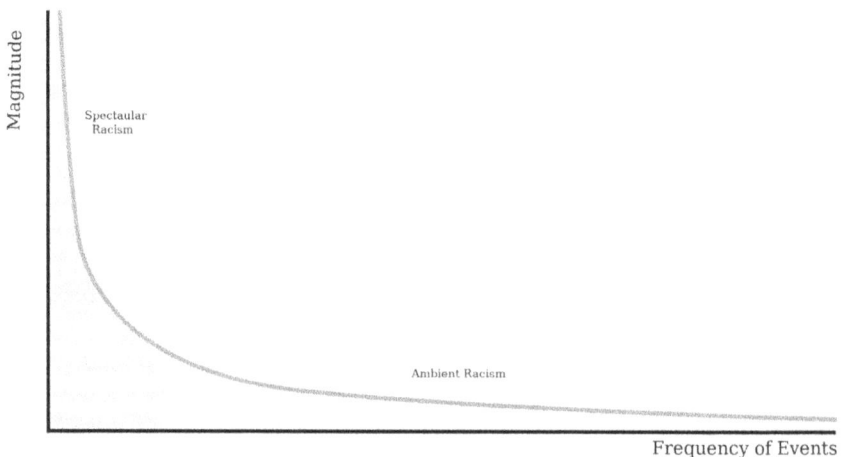

Figure 3.1   **Power Law Distribution.**

book sales and movie profits, citation of academic articles and growth of cities. Famously, the economist, Vilfredo Pareto observed the distribution of wealth following a type of power law named after him, with 80 percent of the wealth being owned by only 20 percent of the population (Bodley 2003).

Surprisingly, given that power laws appear to be present in many kinds of situations, accounting for *why* this distribution occurs is not straightforward (Ladyman et al. 2013). One reason is that power laws arise in *complex systems* comprised of multiple elements (high variance), collectively interacting in a disordered manner through which aggregate and ordered patterns emerge. This characteristic of collective or *emergent* behaviour in a system is 'complex' because it is different from its individual elements – more than the sum of its constituent parts.

More specifically, a power law operates in social information systems or networks which are 'friction-less' and 'non-linear', as described by Srinath Srinivasa (2018):

> A frictionless system is one where transaction costs are extremely low. Because of this, any event in the system is likely to cause a large number of transactions. Frictionless systems are prone to what are called 'non-linearity' in their behaviour. In intuitive terms, this simply means that events and their repercussions are so finely intertwined that it is often impossible to ascertain what is cause and what is effect. Not only do actions cause consequences, the consequences in turn influence the same action further on (15).

Srinivasa points out that the behaviour of friction-less, non-linear systems is usually hard to model, and the forms of networked *connectivity* and scope of variance are crucial in determining the relationship between individual elements and a system's emergent behaviour. In conventional 'linear' systems, variance is restricted and feedback has limited influence, resulting in interactions of elements being more stable and predictable. In comparison, friction-less information systems are characterized by high variance, relatively 'un-damped' feedback which can produce significant, though less predictable impact.

The phenomena of friction-less systems are not merely an abstract idea, but a reality motivating the development of corporate digital platforms. As early as 1995, Bill Gates identified the benefits of 'friction-free capitalism', which has influenced the design of social media platforms.

> Of all the buzzwords in tech, perhaps none has been deployed with as much philosophical conviction as 'frictionless.' Over the past decade or so, eliminating 'friction' [. . .] has become an obsession of the tech industry, accepted as gospel by many of the world's largest companies. (Roose, cite in Tomalin 2018, 5)

In friction-less systems, individual elements or events are interdependent through their interactions. And a key feature is that a small change can give rise to sudden or larger disproportionate changes, independent of the size or quantity of the initial element or event. Power laws, also known as 'scaling laws' or characterizing 'scale-free' distributions operating in friction-less environments, reveal this property of complex, networked systems: 'the changes between phenomena at different scales is independent of which particular scales we are looking at . . . This self-similar property underlies power law relationships' (Bar-Yam 2011).

I contend that it is possible to conceive online racism via the characteristics of a power law (long-tail) distribution. 'Just as normal distributions arise from many independent random decisions averaging out . . .power laws arise from the feedback introduced by correlated decisions across a population' (Easley and Kleinberg 2010, 547). Racism does not occur as an individualized, independent phenomenon. It is embedded in socio-material relations, whether on- or off-line. A racialized event can emerge on social media platforms due to many different interacting and interdependent elements or events such as liking, retweeting, commenting, hashtags, and influenced by various feedback mechanisms such as sharing, newsfeeds, trending and recommendation algorithms, bots and interface design.

Scale, power laws and assemblages can help to unravel the flows and entanglements between racist events of differing scale on networked platforms; in particular, the significance of racialized 'micro' events and their relationship with 'viral' or explosive 'macro' events. Nick Fox and Pam Alldred (2015) elaborate on multi-scalar assemblages when they highlight:

> There is nothing to prevent a relation conventionally thought of as 'micro' . . . and a 'macro' relation . . . to be drawn into assemblage by an affective flow; consequently, an assemblage may contain disparate elements from these different levels (402).

I should stress that a power law distribution is presented as a heuristic figure which offers a means to make sense of the multifarious modalities of online racism that exist in hyper-connected systems.[8] I am not claiming that online racism exhaustively or empirically exhibits the scaling properties of a power law distribution. Rather, it is adopted as a *methodological device* to understand the dynamics of online racism.

Power laws are commonly visualized in terms of the distinction between the head of the distribution and its long tail. Although the demarcation is rather arbitrary, because the distribution is defined by a continuously decreasing function (Shirky 2003). Nonetheless, it is useful to offer an analytical separation between the head and long tail, to map out what I identify as two key scales of online racism: (i) *spectacular racism* located at the head of the distribution and (ii) *ambient racism* residing in the long tail (figure 3.1).

Spectacular Racism

Racialized events which garner significant public *attention* characterize spectacular racism. The head of the power law distribution represents a concentration of power (Herod 2011), which can take the form of high visibility, magnitude, viscerality and impact of a spectacular racialized event. For example, a well-known politician or celebrity expresses a controversial opinion about immigrants or spews a racist outburst, which is explosively shared across social media platforms and news sites. Or a spectacularized event is expressed in the form of a 'viral' video of police shooting an unarmed black civilian; or a trending hashtag or popular meme.

Spectacular racialized events are propagated by a digital 'attention economy' of platform capitalism (Srnicek 2017). A primary means of how these platforms accrue vast profits is through generating advertising revenue (operating as advertising brokers), dependent on maximizing user engagement. The more a user interacts on a platform (posting, reading, scrolling, liking, clicking, retweeting, etc.) the longer time they spend, leading to greater opportunities to monetize their transactional data.

The attention economy operates in an age of information overload, and corporate social media platforms are in competition to gain user attention. As early as 1969, Herbert Simon identified *attention* as a scarce resource: 'the wealth of information means a dearth of something else – a scarcity of whatever it is that information consumes. What information consumes is rather obvious: it consumes the attention of its recipients' (Simon, cited in Citton 2017, 6). Yves Citton stresses that attention is more than individual, we need to consider its collective (and transindividual) formations. The attention of others – what he calls the 'collective attentional regime' – is vital in shaping what we pay attention to.

The design of social media platforms captivates users by creating a networked, friction-less information sharing environment, while essentially disregarding the veracity of content being circulated. Machine-learning recommendation algorithms are at the centre of developing a 'collective attentional regime', innovated by companies such as Alphabet (Google), Twitter, Meta (Facebook) and ByteDance. These recommendation systems dynamically organize and determine which content users are exposed to, as presented in feeds and timelines (Bucher 2012). Many contemporary recommendation systems use 'collaborative filtering' to predict the preference of a user by learning from their and other users' online interactions. This is based on the assumption that users who share similar preferences are likely to agree in the future. That is, recommendations made for you are influenced by other users who have similar tastes to you.

The YouTube video-sharing platform, with currently over 2.6 billion users worldwide, is described by developers at Google as 'one of the largest-scale and most sophisticated industrial recommendation systems in existence' (Covington et al. 2016, 1). These developers recognize that *correctly* recommending videos (personalization) to billions of individual users is challenging, especially because of the enormous user base, vast corpus of dynamically updating videos and the difficulty of predicting user behaviour due to noise in feedback signals. To address this challenge, Paul Covington *et al.* have been involved in pioneering deep neural network architectures ('Google Brain') to develop recommendation algorithms: 'Our models learn approximately one billion parameters and are trained on hundreds of billions of examples' (2016, 1).

YouTube personalized recommendation uses a two-stage deep learning collaborative filtering system. The first stage, 'candidate generation' is based on events from user's history by retrieving a small subset of videos from a larger corpus and provides a broad personalization. The second stage, 'ranking' is more precise, assigning a score to each video by using a vastly richer set of features. 'The two-stage approach to recommendation allows us to make recommendations from a very large corpus (millions) of videos while still being certain that the small number of videos appearing on the device are personalized and engaging for the user' (Covington et al. 2016, 2).

The white paper by Covington *et al.* presents recommendation as a *technical* challenge, governed by the goal of *engaging the user*. However, algorithmically maximizing user engagement has led to unforeseen consequences in how recommendation systems perform in practice. YouTube has been scrutinized for mainstreaming inflammatory and 'extremist' content, including boosting the visibility of QAnon conspiracy theories and racist far-right videos (Nicas 2018; Ribeiro et al. 2020). Based on the investigative work of the software engineer Guillaume Chaslot (fired by Google), Zeynep Tufekci (2018) reported that the 'algorithm seems to have concluded that people are drawn to content that is more extreme than what they started with – or to incendiary content in general.' The attraction towards incendiary or sensational media content is not a new social phenomena. Though, in the era of digital communications, this kind of basest human behaviour has been accelerated and exploited at scale. Journalists at Buzzfeed News fittingly conclude that YouTube's recommendation system is 'an engagement monster' (O'Donovan et al. 2019).

Maximizing engagement 'through affective economies of attention' has also been a hallmark of the video-sharing platform TikTok (Grandinetti and Bruinsma 2022). TikTok massively grew its user base during the global impact of COVID-19 and was one of the most downloaded mobile phone apps during the last decade (Sensor Tower 2020). Developed by the Chinese company ByteDance, TikTok (based on Douyin) brought lip-sync videos, dance challenges and an endless supply of memes into the homes of millions of online users at the height of the pandemic restrictions.

Arvind Narayanan's (2022) discussion of recommendation systems focuses on the innovatory design of TikTok. In comparison to YouTube, TikTok makes it easier for users to be content creators, and appears more equitable in making this content visible: 'What TikTok lacks in superstars it more than makes up for in its "long tail" of creators.' Although TikTok's recommendation system has been accused of suppressing the work of black creators while promoting the cultural appropriation of prevalent white users. Moreover, collaborative filtering can 'reproduce whatever bias there is in people's behaviour. People who tend to like blonde teens tend to like a whole lot of other blonde teens' (Faduol, cited in Strapagiel 2020).

Beyond the discrepant impact of its recommendation system, Narayanan attributes TikTok's mainstream popularity to three design features: the short video form; vertical viewing on mobile devices; and 'swiping' (rather than scrolling).

> On TikTok, swiping up is so quick that you don't consciously notice. So even if YouTube's and TikTok's algorithms are equally accurate, it will feel much more accurate on TikTok . . . Eliminating conscious decision-making from the user experience means that videos that cater to our basest impulses do relatively well on TikTok. (Narayanan 2022)

The TikTok platform is regularly reproached for frenetically spreading dis-information and harmful content such as right-wing extremism, offensive 'black-face' and 'yellow-face' videos (Gorwa et al. 2020; Weimann and Masri 2020). Its failure to implement effective moderation practices is of no surprise for a platform designed to affectively engineer virality and *spectacularize* content.[9]

My focus on the 'spectacular', alongside other media theorists, takes inspiration from Guy Debord's (1967/2012) provocative treatise, *The Society of the Spectacle*. Debord wrote, 'The spectacle is not a collection of images, but a social relation among people mediated by images' (4). He contends that life is fundamentally being experienced through mediated commodified representations, and that individuals are separated (alienated) from every aspect of their lives (e.g. work, leisure, face-to-face interactions). 'Spectacles' create an illusion of freedom rather than revealing how we are exploited by capitalism in modern consumer societies.

Douglas Kellner (2017) in his account of 'spectacles' updates Debord by focusing on media-driven spectacular events. Kellner highlights these spectacles as *exceptional* in the sense that they are experienced differently from more mundane mediations of reality: 'By "media spectacles" I am referring to media constructs that present events which disrupt ordinary and habitual flows of information' (2). Spectacles in a hyper-connected world swiftly appear (and disappear), leading to flash-points, contestations and possibilities of social transformation.

> In a globally networked society, media spectacles proliferate instantaneously, become virtual and viral, and in some cases, becomes tools of socio-political transformation, while other media spectacles become mere moments of media hype and tabloidized sensationalism. (Kellner 2017, 2)

The spectacular rallying cry of Black Lives Matter (BLM) was remarkable for galvanizing protests across many parts of the world. According to the movement's own narrative, #BlackLivesMatter was founded on social media, after the acquittal of George Zimmerman over his shooting of the unarmed Trayvon Martin in 2013. BLM 'moved to the streets' through its involvement in organizing public protests and solidarity rallies against racist police violence and killing of black people (King 2015). BLM exposed the everyday racist violence and death-making force of militarized policing. It centred the daily realities of black communities from an inclusive perspective, recognizing intersectional differences. BLM promoted a radical abolitionist agenda for social transformation.

Notwithstanding the multiracial character of BLM demonstrations, David Leonard and Lisa Guerrero (2013) maintained that media 'spectacularizing of racialized events and tragedies' intensifies the consumption and commodification of black death. The spectacle of the killing of Trayvon Martin disregarded the humanity of black life and found pleasure in suffering of others. Furthermore, Noble (2014) highlights how the *post-racial* media spectacle over Martin's death unctuously renders *race hyper-visible* and *racism invisible*. The trial of Zimmerman and representations of Martin were commodified via the spectacularizing circuits of an attention economy 'to bring about news ratings, increased advertising, and social media traffic at the expense of a national conversation about racial justice' (12). The dominant narrative of black criminality prevailed, with Trayvon Martin embodying hyper-visible blackness as a threat to white society, while at the same time the media spectacle obscured ideologies of racism and erased histories of violence against people of colour.

The death of George Floyd, brutally killed by police in 2020, follows a similar pattern of the spectacularizing of racialized events. A police officer (later found guilty) killed George Floyd by kneeling on his neck for almost ten minutes while handcuffed and pleading for his life. A mobile phone video recording of the death 'went viral', catalysing national and global BLM-led protests. The witnessing of police killing black people being instantly shared via social media has painfully become all too common; as was the case for the deaths of Alton Sterling, Philando Castile, Terrence Crutcher and Eric Garner. One the one hand, these events led to greater public awareness and mobilizations challenging the deadly force of racist police violence. Yet on the other hand, the 'video of Floyd's killing was played ad nauseam online and on TV, retraumatizing his family and community members . . . [O]nce again a Black person killed at the hands of the police is turned into a spectacle' (Reta 2021).

Not only has the *anger* and resistance over the killing of black people been spectacularized, it is being usurped by an 'outrage industry' (Berry and Sobieraj 2014). The affective force of black anger has a long history of collectively mobilizing against racial violence, exclusion and injustice. In contrast, the *post-racial* stoking of outrage – routinely by right-wing actors – feeds a social media economy of attention by indiscriminately 'politicizing everything', and debasing veritable expressions of collective grievance and resistance.

Furthermore, what has pejoratively come to be known as 'cancel culture' (or relatedly 'call-out' culture) is rooted in black cultural resistance and refusal (Mishan 2020). Yet it is deliberately being dispossessed of its criticality and hijacked by an attention economy. The playing out of 'cancel culture' on social media platforms is fraught and often double-edged. There are numerous incidents of public figures being exposed and held to account for something racist they said or did. Practices of 'calling out' racism can be effective in revealing its prevalence in society, if we consider the concern, as Tressie M. Cottom (2014) foregrounds: 'when is a person also a role or an agent of structural violence?' Although the greater the attention, the more rapidly such incidents risk being spectacularized, and spiral into social media 'dragging' or facile *ad hominem* attacks (Benjamin 2019). At the same time, these events are routinely met with responses of denial, which obfuscate racial hierarchies and power: 'racism is framed as an exceptional outburst and treated as an individual aberration, not only unconnected from any broader political or systemic patterns, but also often "repudiated publicly so that the routine activities of racist statecraft may continue"' (Titley 2019, 6).

Racialized spectacles are reduced to 'outbreaks' (see part I), articulated via a *post-racial* fabrication that confounds possibilities of understanding and social transformation. The digital attention economy is indifferent to whether user engagement produces meaningful, fallacious or adversarial interactions. Forms of spectacular racism are presented as endless series of capricious events, to be reported and virally circulated, made *visible* supposedly for the public good. Yet media spectacularization banalizes racist events as sensational and exceptional.

Ambient Racism

Spectacular racism located at the head of a power law distribution largely defines how racism is made publicly visible and un/intelligible. If we consider the inordinate flows of social media information (text, images, videos, comments, likes, etc.), what becomes visible to wider publics is not easy to anticipate. Only a small fraction of the enormous volume of online interactions ever surface to be *noticed* (cf. Lovink 2007). The digital attention economy is designed to engineer 'virality' in the face of the info-deluge of contemporary media flows. Arguably, what becomes visible follows the characteristics of the distribution of a power law. While 'macro' events at the head of the tail are relatively rare in comparison to 'micro' events of the long tail, nonetheless, they have far more dramatic social impact.

It is tempting to assume that events occurring in the long tail are inconsequential in comparison to highly visible spectacular events. Consider for a moment, the streams of everyday tweets harbouring racial slurs, insults and 'micro-aggressions'. Most will have only a tiny reach, never be seen, liked or retweeted and will fall by the wayside. These individual 'micro' events, while far more numerous than what occurs at the head of the tail, lack visibility and *appear* to have little, if any, impact or traction.

There are legitimate reasons why most academic research attention focus on highly visible racialized events. Power laws suggest that these events have disproportionate impact across online and off-lines spaces, and can reinforce existing structures of power (cf. Herod 2011). Whether it is the police killing black civilians or the relentless harassment of women of colour on social media platforms, these abhorrent events are symptomatic of endemic forms of racism. Nonetheless, Benjamin (2019) points to the problem of allowing 'more obvious forms of virulent racism to monopolize our attention, when the equivalent of slow death – the subtler and even alluring forms of coded inequity – get a pass' (24).

In comparison, researching racist micro-events in the long tail appears labyrinthine. Such events are multifarious in form and content, and likely to be fleeting, sporadic and indirect. For example, tracking the evolution of how an innocuous single image is shared, and then mutates over time into a humorous or ambiguous racially coded meme via a chain of ordinary and hostile actors is challenging to analyse. It is usually only feasible to study *after* the meme has surfaced and become visible (recall the 'Pepe the Frog' meme discussed in part I).

From a perspective of scale, we should avoid assuming that the less visible events of the long tail are inconsequential or have negligible impact. The significance of the long tail was popularized for commerce by Chris Anderson (2006), who argued that the *aggregated* sales of less popular items (residing in the long tail) could be larger than those generated by the head of the distribution. Anderson dwelt on quantity and volume characterizing the long tail. He was influenced by the earlier essay by Clay Shirky (2003), 'Power Laws, Weblogs and Inequality'. Shirky focused on exploring the seemingly ineffable characteristic of the skewed power law distribution of user preferences in 'unconstrained social systems'.

Earlier, I highlighted that in 'friction-less' information systems, individual events are interdependent through their interactions. Following on, it is appropriate to ask, how do we understand the 'impact' of online racist micro-events? In relation to scale, it is not only about numerical aggregation, such as when enough micro-events converge or transform into a spectacular macro-event. What is more difficult to grasp is the influence or impact of events *inhabiting* the long tail which appear isolated, banal and insignificant. By briefly turning to two research studies I was involved in, we can identify the 'ambient' characteristics of a racism of the long tail.

The first study examined the everyday practices of the denial of racism on the Twitter platform (Sharma and Brooker 2016). A post-racial condition has empowered users to say racist things while refuting any malicious intent, as expressed by the sentiment *'I'm not racist, but . . .'*. Although to capture racism denial on social media platforms is tricky because it can be communicated in ambiguous and coded ways, as expressed by the tweets:

I Hate Basketball & Rap Music #notracist
I literally cant stop eating watermelon. And Im not even black #notracist

When exploring Twitter, it was discovered that the hashtag *#notracist* was used to punctuate a user's tweet (a declarative stance of racism denial). The *#notracist* hashtag tended not to be about any specific event or controversy. The study collected a dataset of almost 25,000 tweets with the hashtag over an 8-month period. As indicated in the tweets above, these messages were diverse in semantic meaning. They were found to be bubbling away on the Twitter platform, as a kind of 'background' chatter or noise without ever trending or becoming markedly visible. Users posting these tweets had few followers, and their fleeting messages were rarely retweeted or liked, effectively remaining 'invisible' – characteristic of the long tail. While the *#notracist* hashtag did not beget significant interactions among dispersed users, its deployment nonetheless intimates a shared sensibility of racism denial. To put it another way, the inclusion of the hashtag suggests an affiliative or *ambient* mode of communication, invoking 'the notion that there are people who feel the same way . . . regardless of the fact that it is unlikely that anyone would ever use the tag as a search term' (Zappavigna 2015, 18).

The ambient can be conceived *affectively* – the musician Brian Eno (1978) describes it as 'an atmosphere, or a surrounding influence. [I]t accommodates many levels of attention . . . without enforcing one in particular'. To elaborate, the ambient can capture how racialized micro-events are dispersed, discontinuous and hidden, yet they create an indiscernible atmosphere of normalization. Clive Thompson highlights a 'paradox of ambient awareness':

> Each little update – each individual bit of social information – is insignificant on its own, even supremely mundane. But taken together, over time, the little snippets coalesce into a surprisingly sophisticated portrait . . . like thousands of dots making a pointillist painting. (Thompson, cited in McCullough 2013, 12)

If the attention economy contributes to propagating forms of online racism, it is worth pointing to its *affective* orbit. Sarah Ahmed's (2004) account of an 'affective economy' highlights how the circulation and flow of emotions connect people together at a distance, and may produce the effect of an emergent collective.

Another research study I collaborated on, investigated the hostility of the comment culture of the YouTube platform (Murthy and Sharma 2019). YouTube is notorious for weakly moderating its comment space (appearing below videos). Our study discovered that antagonistic comments were 'networked', and far from merely random or fleeting insults. The forms of expression could be 'troll-like constructive/destructive, humorous/offensive and serious/banal . . . apocryphal or ambivalent and entangled alongside other antagonistic and non-antagonistic commentary' (209).

While it is common to point to the most vitriolic and visible expressions of hate on the YouTube platform, in reality, these are often entangled with trolling or more mundane, demotic forms of hostility and everyday cursory insults. What became apparent was an economy of racialized affects influencing the behaviour of users: 'not only are there emotional investments in the making of comments, these are also animated and charged by racial antagonisms that *connect* users to networked spaces of communication' (208). While many comments appeared isolated with little response, other comments spawned more complicated interactions among users that were difficult to unravel and make sense of. These passed through multiple parts of the comment space, unfolding affective networked interactions which created a generalized or 'ambient' culture of disaccord on the platform.

Ambient racism is difficult to pin down, because of its seemingly impalpable, environmental qualities. It can come across as operating in the background, yet its *scale* can have significant impact. In 'friction-less' systems small events can generate larger effects. This does not ignore how impactful 'broadcast events' – propagated by a hub or authority, operating at the head of the power law distribution – are directly involved in producing highly visible racialized events on social media platforms (cf. Kucharski 2020). Nor does it disregard how forms of spectacular racism create the conditions for, and legitimate, everyday cultures of online infraction. Rather, the significance of ambient-events acknowledges they play a critical role in circulating racialized affects. These affective flows give rise to racially charged atmospheres and precipitate palpable forms of spectacular racism. Although as mentioned, in reality spectacular and ambient forms of racism are troublesome to conceptually and operationally disentangle. Eugenia Siapera (2019) in a study exploring racialized public discourse maintains that these distinctions do not hold, and 'analysis shows that both ambient and organized/extreme forms co-exist and mutually reinforce one another' (26).

Nonetheless, more intangible to fathom and more likely to be overlooked are the *enduring* effects of ambient racism. That is, to recognize the impact of countless racially charged micro-events which people of colour experience on a daily basis. While these online events are not spectacularized, they remain pervasive and damaging. A case in point is the common occurrence of so-called 'micro-aggressions' on social media platforms. From a typical psychological hate-prejudice standpoint, micro-aggressions are reductively framed in terms of flawed individual behaviour; interpersonal acts that are incidental and distinct events. In contrast, from a systemic racism standpoint, individuals mediate societal and structural forms of racism via acts of micro-aggression (Essed 1991; Syed 2021). Analysing 'everyday racism' Philomena Essed pointed to its invisibility and normalization, and how its pernicious effects accumulate over time. Remarkably, the 'cumulative effects' of micro-aggressions can have as much (and possibly more) impact than overt forms of racism. Kirsten Jones et al. (2016) highlight this phenomenon when they discuss the differences of subtle (micro) and overt (macro) forms of discrimination:

> subtle discrimination may be more damaging for targets because of its higher frequency and thus the chronic nature of its effects. Indeed, extant research has argued that one reason for the particularly damaging impact of subtle discrimination lies in its pervasiveness, whereas overt discriminatory behavior may occur less often. (1590)

Scale informs us that ambient racism is more than the sum of its constituent parts. It is important to reiterate that the 'cumulative effects' or 'chronic nature' of micro-events are not simply the adding-up of incidents, which could go onto produce a momentous impact. Alternatively, Rob Nixon (2011) examines the notion of 'slow violence' and asks how we grasp 'threats that take time to wreak their havoc, threats that never materialize in one spectacular, explosive . . . scene' (14). It may well be that ambient racism is an *emergent* form of 'slow violence' that remains diffuse and hidden (for some), but is insidious and attritional over time and space (Davies 2022).

The 'slow violence' of ambient racism can take other forms. What has been described as the 'slow red-pill' is an insidious, covert tactic that has been deployed by the Alt/far-right (Citarella 2021). Rather than immediately posting extreme and overtly racist content, more common conservative-leaning viewpoints are initially expressed and circulated on social media platforms. This can lead to building up an audience over time, and then these users are gradually exposed to more extreme and spectacular racist opinions and material. While Big Tech platforms lacked volition to moderate harmful content and struggled to moderate 'spectacular' racist online content, identifying and curtailing ambient forms of racism poses an even greater challenge.

The concept of *scale* can help us to understand how social media platforms function as racializing assemblages. Scale unpacks the multiplicity of online racism(s), revealing that different elements have varying degrees of influence, with diverse impacts. The ways in which different scalings interact is valuable for grasping the post-racial, multi-modality of online racism. Most attention is paid to highly visible 'spectacular' racialized events. Yet it has been argued that less visible, 'ambient' events are as significant. While these transient infractions are not immediately impactful, their accumulative effects can elusively induce an atmosphere of legitimizing and proliferating forms of online racism.

Understanding the multi-modality of online racism has involved innovating an interdisciplinary framework. By presenting an account of scale, via assemblage theory and power laws, a *particular* approach to addressing the post-racial complexity of social media racism has been developed. Identifying the scalings of 'spectacular' and 'ambient' are two kinds of framings (and still may risk reproducing 'macro' and 'micro' thinking). To veritably address and analyse the sociotechnical entanglements of digital racism is not only a challenging concern, but one that necessitates creative methodological thinking.

NOTES

1. I explore 'online racism' with a focus on 'social media platforms'. Online spaces (or the 'web') include platforms, though also refer other digital environments such as chat rooms, web forums, gaming and virtual reality sites. In practice, it can be difficult to disentangle online spaces from social media platforms, because the latter as infrastructures have become dominant in defining and controlling how we interact on the internet.

2. There is of course a range of work exploring web-based racism pre-dating the rise of social media, for discussions of key studies, see especially Daniels (2013), and Nakamura and Chow-White (2011). Notable studies focusing on social media racism include Chun (2021), Matamoros-Fernández (2017), Siapera (2019) and Titley (2019). For a systematic review, see Matamoros-Fernández and Farkas (2021).

3. I would like to thank colleagues at CIM, Michael Castelle and Emma Uprichard, for discussing ideas about Scale.

4. Since the publication of the study, further research has confirmed the rise of volumes of hate speech, see for example Williams (2021).

5. We should not confuse 'ordinary' racism with how Richard Delgado and Jean Stefancic (2017) use this term. In their account, racism is 'ordinary' in the sense it is not a social aberration, but a normalized, common experience of most people of colour.

6. The GIFT became a popular meme in the form of a cartoon graphic, originally appearing on the 'Penny Arcade' (2004) comic website. For a more detailed account of its history, see the entry on the 'Know Your Meme' (2012) website.

7. Arturo Escobar (2007) makes a similar point about assemblages and scale when he writes: 'There is recurrence of the same assembly process at a given spatial scale, and recurrence at successive scales, leading to a different conceptualization of the link between the micro and the macro levels of social reality' (108).

8. For instance, Broido and Clasuet (2019) state that the 'universality of scale-free networks . . . remains controversial' (2).

9. Zulli and Zulli (2022) in their discussion of 'technological memesis' contend that 'TiKTok extends the Internet meme to the level of platform infrastructure' (1973).

Epilogue

The essential *race-making* capacity of digital technologies has been a key concern of this book. Racism has existed prior to the rise of digital technologies. We could conclude that until *societal* racism is surmounted, digital forms of racism will persist. But this way of thinking echoes the belief that the 'real' and 'virtual' are distinct domains, and the former is determinate of the latter. Strongly bifurcating the social and technological has little credibility in contemporary studies of digital technologies. Nonetheless, when studying technological-based forms of racism, it is not easy to offer perspectives that altogether avoid social (or conversely technological) forms of determinism. It is from this problematic, ideas for this book have developed. I have maintained that understanding digital racism remains stalled unless we explore its *sociotechnical entanglements*.

The entangled interactions of the social and technological can lead to *emergent post-racial* forms of digital racism, which are difficult to grasp and anticipate. Digital technologies are proliferating and transforming racism, complicating our understanding and making contemporary racism increasingly harder to challenge. This is not only because of the sociotechnical complexity and generative force of racializing technologies. It is also because digital racism is constituted via a *post-raciality* able to evade, contest and undermine meaningful political analysis and scrutiny. Moreover, the condition of post-raciality marks the acceleration and intensification of racial transformations. To say that digital racism is multitudinous and multifarious barely captures its contemporary motilities and mutations. In other words, the problems of digital racism are manifold, and there aren't any simple 'fixes' or solutions.

The histories of racism and technology are deeply entangled (Benjamin 2019; Eubanks 2018). The use of ships, navigation instruments and guns enabled the transatlantic slave trade. Racial classification and the Eugenics movement were predicated on medical instruments and advances in statistics. Mapping technologies in urban areas have been used to 'redline' and exclude black populations and access to resources. AI-based facial recognition surveillance target and mis-identify people of colour. Not only are such technologies of control profoundly racialized, but equally there has been a long history of people of colour *resisting* these technologies (Browne 2015).

When technologies of control widen their ambit and begin to affect *the majority* – white and more privileged populations – then the potential social harms of technology gain greater public recognition and opposition (Benjamin 2019; Noble 2017). Notably, the mainstreaming of this recognition can neglect or occlude acknowledging the histories of people of colour challenging technologies of control. For example, the public calls to ban automated facial recognition across Western nations, are largely framed in individualist human rights/privacy discourse. These calls invariably fail to address the histories of collective, anti-racist struggles against policing and violence.

This *Epilogue* explores resisting and overcoming digital racism. What I raise addresses *wider* concerns, which appear to be beyond the immediate racializing impact of digital technologies. Though as argued, it is not possible to disentangle racism from technological advances. Thus, *anti-racist resistance* is not marginal but *cardinal* to broader struggles against the expansion and intensification of corporate and state technologies of data extraction and control across society. I offer a set of four provocations, to spur further critical thinking and bring about possibilities for change. These are by no means prescriptive, as *tactics* (de Certeau 1984) they are to be forged through struggle and everyday practices. The concerns raised are in dialogue with, and inspired by, other scholars working in this field – see especially Benjamin (2019). By identifying and bringing together differing ways of thinking and tactics, the aim is to direct our collective efforts to counter digital racism.

1. BEYOND BREAKING UP BIG TECH

Big Tech has colonized the internet, largely determining how we participate and interact online. The capitalist strategies of digital dispossession and data extraction pursue corporate profit over any other concerns. This has been achieved by an 'attention economy' maximizing user engagement on digital platforms, via engineering hyper-connectivity and virality of content. The propagation of dis-information, racism and other intersectional oppressions effectively operate as a *feature* of online environments arbitrated by Big Tech. Their dire attempts at ethical conduct and content moderation can be likened to applying sticking plasters to a system defective-by-design.

Currently, Big Tech of the Global North – Google/Alphabet, Apple, Face-book/Meta and Microsoft (GAFAM) – are valued at $5 trillion. Their profits topped 320 billion dollars in 2021, bolstered during the COVID-19 pandemic (Kwet 2020; Poletti and Owens 2022). The 'techlash' calls to break up the Big Tech ecosystem have reached the U.S. Congress, highlighting the anti-competitive business practices of these technology behemoths. However, this antitrust agenda mainly embraces reforming capitalism to restore greater market competition (a perspective remarkably supported by Zuboff's (2019) critique of surveillance capitalism).

Breaking up Big Tech is only a step in the right direction by reclaiming and developing alternative digital infrastructures and communication cultures beyond profit and control-driven agendas. This could involve building a 'public service internet' that benefits society as a whole, rather than corporate interests determined by an 'attention economy' (see Fuchs and Unterberger 2021). More radically, the 'Non-Aligned Technologies Movement' (NATM) addresses concerns of digital self-determination and governance by communities:

> NATM would create parallel platforms to those offered by the Big Tech axis, but without the extraction and dispossession. These platforms would cease to be niche solutions explored by hacker communities, but widely used solutions that offer non-aligned members alternatives to Big Tech. (Mejias 2020)

Needless to say, it is not easy to develop alternative infrastructures and communication cultures. The discussion below continues to explore how these may be realized.

2. 'MOVE SLOW AND BUILD THINGS'?

For many years, the Silicon Valley ideology of disruptive technologies as a determinant of social progress was aggrandized by Facebook founder Mark Zuckerberg's infamous maxim, 'move fast and break things'. The domination of Big Tech over the digital landscape can be attributed to a culture of innovating quickly and taking risks for rapid growth. Zukerberg's maxim has been recast – 'move fast and build infra[structure]' – in response to greater public recognition of possible social harms caused by reckless technological innovation. (Although the tenants of the 'attention economy' business models of Big Tech prevail.)

Often overlooked in accounts of the imperious idea of 'move fast and break things', is its dubious connections to neo-reactionary 'accelerationist' ideologies that push for the ceaseless speeding up and intensification of capitalism, technology and automation (MacKay and Avanessian 2014). Disturbingly, white supremacists, including some who have gone on to commit mass shootings, have broadcast neo-reactionary and accelerationist 'reasoning' via social media platforms (Beauchamp 2019). More generally, accelerationist thought has influenced the Alt-Right and Alt-Tech focus on, and use of, technology. The mainstreaming of 'extremist' viewpoints (shifting the Overton window) by harnessing and manipulating digital communication platforms, is symptomatic of the Alt/far-right seeking to precipitate the demise of liberal democracy and sow social discord.

In response to the speed and exploitability of digital platforms, the over-consumption of information and 'addictive' design of social media and apps, there have been various counter efforts such as 'time well spent' (Centre for Humane Technology) and 'slow media' (Köhler et al. 2010; Rauch 2018). These call for reducing our dependency on digital media through practices of digital detoxing or disconnection, or creating sustainable media technologies, and less reactive and more 'mindful' communication cultures. While 'slow media' thinking has gained popularity, it largely remains individualist and lacks a structural critique able to confront the hegemony of Big Tech (Ganesh 2018).

Nonetheless, decelerating digital culture coupled with alternative 'de-scaled' communication infrastructures could be a way forward, especially to address the toxicity of social media. As a case, we can take a brief look at the Twitter social media platform. Twitter shares the accelerationist logics of speed and intensity. Although it is a contested space, circulating dis-information, conspiracy theories and 'hate-speech', while simultaneously (and unintentionally?) enabling socially progressive activism and radical formations such as 'Black Twitter' to emerge (Brock 2020).

The acquisition of Twitter in 2022 by the controversial entrepreneur, Elon Musk, reveals the brittleness of propriety social platforms media that have appropriated spaces for public discourse – 'our commons'. In the pursuit of profit and efficiency, Musk has dismissed many Twitter employees, including 'Trust and Safety' staff (Zakrzewski 2022). In response to the takeover, some Twitter users have migrated to the open-source platform Mastodon.

Mastodon is part of the 'fediverse', thousands of independent servers interacting using standard open protocols. The Mastodon platform has some noteworthy features: Decentralization – not owned or controlled by a central authority; Community-based – users can deploy their own servers or 'instances' leading to greater autonomy; Federated – ability to control connections to the wider network of other 'instances', and; Content visibility – not algorithmically determined by an 'attention economy'.

A key characteristic of Mastodon is how it 'scales'. In this regard, it has not been designed or intended to replace Twitter. In comparison to corporate social media, Mastodon is based on an alternative set of values and practices. A federated structure offers the potential to 'scale' differently – in contrast to being governed by a single, centralized authority that amasses a user base and subjects them to algorithmically ordered content (Zulli et al. 2020). Mastodon and other decentralized platforms of the fediverse have greater *friction* in their overall design. Implementing friction in the use and affordances of social media platforms has been deployed to slow down the spread of dis-information and hate-speech. For Twitter, a user can control who can see or reply to a tweet. Increasing public and regulatory pressure has forced corporate social media platforms to introduce types of friction to limit content sharing, by tweaking their interface design. Although it is not always apparent or consistent on what basis content is automatically marked as suspect or is subject to being blocked (White et al. 2022).

In comparison, friction is far more systemic in Mastodon. For example, the message of a user posting on their 'instance' is not necessarily seen by users on another instance (depending on where their followers are located, use of hashtags, or if the instance has a 'federated timeline'). Finding other users on Mastodon, who may be on different 'instances' involves far more effort than on Twitter. Mastodon users have greater control in who they interact with. An administrator can decide on the visibility and user access of their instance, as well as which other instances are connected to in the fediverse.

Alternative social media infrastructures and technical design affordances do not infallibly lead to liberatory spaces of communication and communities, free of racism. People of colour and other marginalized groups on Mastodon have experienced racist abuse and harassment (Fowler 2022; Star 2023). Johnathan Flowers (2022) reminds us that the development of alternative platforms is not outside of the enduring histories of racism and whiteness.

> Mastodon is a very white space. It draws upon some of the values and some of the interests of indie web producers, of the DIY tech community, wherein there's this sense of rugged individualism [. . .] It is not unlike other tech spaces where whiteness is predominant. Insofar as this is the case, the norms, the habits, the affordances of the platform will inherit whiteness.

Flowers also highlights that the affordances of Mastodon can make it challenging to form connections and social relations across the fediverse. This may make it less likely that a 'Black Twitter' type of formation can flourish on Mastodon. Additionally, Flowers points to the financial challenges of running 'instances of colour', and the labour involved moderating against racist harassment. And in the context of an extant racist society, a federated structure can 'have an entire instance of right-wing white supremacists pop up that would engage in targeted harassment of users of color' (Flowers 2022).

In comparison to being entirely dependent on the centralized authority of corporate platforms to curtail harassment, arguably there is more autonomy for Mastodon administrators to intervene. The feature of *defederation* enables a whole instance to be blocked (Star 2023). When the so-called 'free speech' Gab social media platform launched in 2016, it first used Mastodon software. But because of its tolerance of hate-speech, harassment and connections with violent white supremacists, Gab was soon isolated from many other Mastodon instances (leading it to effectively leave the fediverse).

To 'move slowly and build things' should not narrowly be framed as a technical solution to tackling the intractability of digital racism. While this kind of design philosophy has the potential to counter the accelerationist logics of corporate social media, it is not a panacea. As will become evident, it also points to issues concerning which values and whose perspectives are included in the development of digital technologies. 'If design is treated as inherently moving forward, that is, as the solution, have we even agreed upon the problem?' (Benjamin 2019, 180).

3. BAN (MOST) AI

In March 2023, the think-tank Future of Life Institute (FLI 2023) co-ordinated the publication of an open letter 'Pause Giant AI Experiments', which declared 'all AI labs to immediately pause for at least 6 months the training of AI systems more powerful than GPT-4'. The letter has thousands of signatories, including Elon Musk, Steve Woznick (Apple co-founder) and Youshua Benigo (Alan Turning award winner), as well as developers from DeepMind, Google, Meta and Microsoft. The letter raised concerns of managing the potential risks of AI in order to benefit society:

> Recent months have seen AI labs locked in an out-of-control race to develop and deploy ever more powerful digital minds that no one – not even their creators – can understand, predict, or reliably control [. . .] Powerful AI systems should be developed only once we are confident that their effects will be positive and their risks will be manageable. (FLI 2023)

The current frenzy over the rapid and widespread deployment of human-like AI conversational chatbots resulted in the letter attracting significant media attention and discussion. In comparison, three years earlier, more than 1,400 mathematicians and data scientists signed a letter calling for their discipline to stop working on predictive policing algorithms. And in response to the continuing police brutality against people of colour, to boycott collaborating with policing organizations in developing these systems (Castelvecchi 2020). The anti-predictive policing letter – pointing to a *present-day* technology targeting racialized communities – received far less attention compared to the FLI publication.

As critics pointed out, the FLI letter is alarmed by a far-fetched, dystopian future of out-of-control 'Super AI', and fails to consider the real harms caused by *current* AI systems deployed in policing, healthcare and social welfare. A rebuttal to the FLI letter from the Distributed AI Research Institute (DAIR), authored by Bender et al. (2021) insists that

> The current race towards ever larger 'AI experiments' is not a preordained path where our only choice is how fast to run, but rather a set of decisions driven by the profit motive. The actions and choices of corporations must be shaped by regulation which protects the rights and interests of people.

The most advanced AI technologies are developed by elite corporations due to the significant resources required in building and training these systems. To date, government regulation of AI has been weak and inadequate. While regulatory efforts to reign in AI may improve, profit and control-driven rationalities are far from aligning with values progressing social equity and justice.

Much of the publicity surrounding the use of AI assumes its societal benefits, while seemingly acknowledging potential harms and pre-empting unintended consequences. Such a contrived acknowledgement remains subordinate to accelerationist ideas of technological disruption, the capitalist drive of wealth accumulation, and surveillant regimes of control. The AI discourse of 'benefits' versus 'future harms' is narrowly framed in terms of a specious trade-off, to ensure technological progress.

Yarden Katz (2020) maintains that AI is not universal or all-purposeful, benefiting society as a whole, rather it 'is a technology of whiteness: malleable, contested, and continually remade to serve imperial and capitalist aims' (226). Continuing this line of critique, Luke Stark (2019), writing about the widespread deployment of AI-based facial recognition systems, offers an alternative framing. Drawing an analogy between the nuclear dangers of plutonium and present-day social harms caused by facial recognition technology, Stark concludes:

> It's dangerous, racializing, and has few legitimate uses; facial recognition needs regulation and control on par with nuclear waste [. . .] Facial recognition's racializing effects are so potentially toxic to our lives as social beings that its widespread use doesn't outweigh the risks (50, 55).

What Stark does is to overturn the so-called trade-off, by foregrounding the extant racializing violence of digital technologies.

If we approach AI as exigently detrimental to society – by centring the racialized and marginalized communities that this technology inexorably impacts upon – then halting the deployment of AI becomes a default position. It is only in specific circumstances that AI be developed, effectively 'sand-boxed' to address particular problems. Admittedly, as long as a global neoliberal techno-social order prevails, to implement and govern a policy to contain AI seems insurmountable. But should that prevent us from imagining and building other possibilities for technology?

4. *SHIFT POWER*

Gil Scott-Heron's brilliant spoken-word song, *Whitey on the Moon* (1970) lambasted the U.S. government for spending billions of dollars sending white people into space, while ignoring the struggles of black Americans against poverty and oppression. It also was a prescient critique of the notion of *progress* regarding the emergence of a techno-military-industrial-academic complex that dominates the development of digital technologies. In the summer of 2021, the song title 'Whitey on the Moon' trended on social media, in response to the space flights of billionaires Richard Branson and Jeff Bezos during the throes of the Covid pandemic and ever-widening global wealth gaps (Dennis 2021).

Scott-Heron's observations about the *intersections* of technology, racial inequity and black alienation alongside his pioneering music, connected him with the expansive cultural movement of 'Afrofuturism' emerging in the 1970s – a term retroactively coined by Mark Dery (1994). Afrofuturism combines science fiction, revolutionary music and innovatory artistic practices. It envisions shaping alternative futures through a 'Black cultural lens', involving reclaiming and re-purposing technology in new ways (Womack 2013). Technology has always been part of the cultural development of people of colour, in spite of being excluded from global innovations. Contemporary Afrofuturism resonates with speculative fiction and abolitionist methods, valuing intervention, experimentation and creativity. These approaches prioritize the agencies of minoritized communities, to ideate alternative possible futures towards social and racial equity (Bray and Harrington 2021).

To advocate re-imagining technology from Afrofuturist and abolitionist critical perspectives is not the same as championing approaches such as 'AI for Social Good' (cf. Katz 2020). As pointed out, these reductive discourses of 'benefits vs harms' are predicated on racial-capitalist-accelerationist values of technological innovation and disruption. Though, can the logics of computational systems be freed from the historical entanglements of racism and technology? Can digital technologies be re-purposed or re-imagined otherwise?

McQuillan (2022) is heedful of the possibilities of re-purposing *existing* technologies because they are designed to determine and solve problems via logics of abstraction, datafication and automation. These systems 'are not simply tools that can be turned to good ends or bad but technosocial infrastructures with an established momentum' (146). He points to how the accelerationist, techno-solutionist drive of 'the exponential scaling of computing power is complicit with the economic ideology of unconstrained growth' (147). If we are to try and advance alternative approaches, these will involve re-imaging the function and purpose of technology beyond solving problems defined on its own terms. McQuillan suggests that when developing an alternative apparatus, 'rather than striving for autonomous computation, it acts as a support for social autonomy' (147).

Furthermore, recent critical race/data justice, abolitionist and decolonial critiques of digital technology evoke Afrofuturist ways of thinking and intervening in the world. The work of Ruha Benjamin (2016) exploring 'speculative fictions' emphasizes experimentation and forging new values:

> that reimagine and rework all that is taken for granted about the current structure of the social world – alternatives to capitalism, racism, and patriarchy – are urgently needed. Fictions [are] refashionings through which analysts experiment with different scenarios, trajectories, and reversals, elaborating new values and testing different possibilities for creating more just and equitable societies (2).

It has been highlighted that by centring the perspectives of groups most impacted by digital systems such as AI, notions of social and technological progress are re-oriented towards the sustenance of minoritized populations. Pratyusha Kalluri (2020) elaborates, by advocating an abolitionist approach that dismantles existing systems of concentrated power, and alternatively to create 'anti-oppressive technologies' to build a better world. Kalluri resoundingly asserts: 'Don't ask if AI is good or fair, ask how it shifts power' (169).

When Audre Lorde (1979) warned that 'the master's tools will never dismantle the master's house'; it was a revolutionary appeal to experiment and reconceive tools to *shift power*. This also calls to engage in struggles to transform the ownership, structures, architectures and knowledge production of technologies (Gilmore 2022). The work of 'shifting power' is already underway. To name just a few, groups such as *Radical AI Network*, *Our Bodies*, *Stop LAPD Spying Coalition* and *BLAST Fest* resist oppressive technologies and seek to empower communities. To overcome and dismantle the many forms of digital racism involves progressing a range of tactics, informed by critical thinking and grounded in everyday life. It goes without saying, re-imagining technology to materialize alternative futures is an ongoing, collective struggle.

Bibliography

Adams, Richard, and Niamh McIntyre. 2020. 'England A-Level Downgrades Hit Pupils from Disadvantaged Areas Hardest'. *The Guardian*. https://www.theguardian.com/education/2020/aug/13/england-a-level-downgrades-hit-pupils-from-disadvantaged-areas-hardest.

Ahmed, Sara. 2004. 'Affective Economies'. *Social Text* 22 (2): 117–39.

Ahuja, Neel. 2018. 'Post-Mortem on Race and Control'. In *Control Culture: Foucault and Deleuze After Discipline*, edited by Frida Beckman, 34–43. Edinburgh: Edinburgh University Press.

Ali, Syed Mustafa. 2019. '"White Crisis" and/as "Existential Risk," or the Entangled Apocalypticism of Artificial Intelligence'. *Zygon* 54 (1): 207–24. https://doi.org/10.1111/zygo.12498.

Amaro, Ramon. 2019a. 'Artificial Intelligence: Warped, Colorful Forms and Their Unclear Geometries'. In *Schemas of Uncertainty: Soothsayers and Soft AI*, edited by Danae Io and Callum Copley, 69–90. Amsterdam: PUB/Sandberg Instituut.

———. 2019b. 'As If'. *E-Flux*. https://www.e-flux.com/architecture/becoming-digital/248073/as-if/.

Amoore, Louise. 2009. 'Algorithmic War: Everyday Geographies of the War on Terror'. *Antipode* 41 (1): 49–69. https://doi.org/10.1111/j.1467-8330.2008.00655.x.

———. 2013. *The Politics of Possibility: Risk and Security beyond Probability*. Durham, NC: Duke University Press.

———. 2020. *Cloud Ethics: Algorithms and the Attributes of Ourselves and Others*. Durham, NC: Duke University Press.

———. 2021. 'The Deep Border'. *Political Geography*. https://doi.org/10.1016/j.polgeo.2021.102547.

Ananny, Mike. 2016. 'Toward an Ethics of Algorithms: Convening, Observation, Probability, and Timeliness'. *Science, Technology, & Human Values* 41 (1): 93–117. https://doi.org/10.1177/0162243915606523.

Ananny, Mike, and Kate Crawford. 2018. 'Seeing Without Knowing: Limitations of the Transparency Ideal and Its Application to Algorithmic Accountability'. *New Media & Society* 20 (3): 973–89. https://doi.org/10.1177/1461444816676645.

Anderson, Chris. 2006. *The Long Tail: Why the Future of Business Is Selling Less of More*. London: Hachette.
———. 2008. 'The End of Theory: The Data Deluge Makes the Scientific Method Obsolete'. *Wired*. https://www.wired.com/2008/06/pb-theory/.
Andrejevic, Mark, Alison Hearn, and Helen Kennedy. 2015. 'Cultural Studies of Data Mining: Introduction'. *European Journal of Cultural Studies* 18 (4–5): 379–94. https://doi.org/10.1177/1367549415577395.
Anti-Defamation League. 2017. 'From 4Chan, Another Trolling Campaign Emerges'. Anti-Defamation League. https://www.adl.org/blog/from-4chan-another-trolling-campaign-emerges.
Atkinson, Robert D., Doug Brake, Daniel Castro, Colin Cunliff, Joe Kennedy, Michael McLaughlin, Alan McQuinn, and Joshua New. 2019. 'A Policymaker's Guide to the "Techlash"'. Information Technology and Innovation Foundation. https://itif.org/publications/2019/10/28/policymakers-guide-techlash.
Azavea. 2014. 'HunchLab: Under the Hood'. Philadelphia, PA: Azavea.
Barabási, Albert-László. 2009. 'Scale-Free Networks: A Decade and Beyond'. *Science* 325 (5939): 412–13. https://doi.org/10.1126/science.1173299.
Barabási, Albert-László, and Eric Bonabeau. 2003. 'Scale-Free Networks'. *Scientific American* 288 (5): 60–69. https://doi.org/10.1038/scientificamerican0503-60.
Baran, Paul. 1964. 'On Distributed Communications Networks'. *IEEE Transactions on Communications Systems* 12 (1): 1–9. https://doi.org/10.1109/TCOM.1964.1088883.
Barbrook, Richard, and Andy Cameron. 1996. 'The Californian Ideology'. *Science as Culture* 6 (1): 44–72. https://doi.org/10.1080/09505439609526455.
Barlow, John Perry. 1996. 'A Declaration of the Independence of Cyberspace'. Electronic Frontier Foundation. https://www.eff.org/cyberspace-independence.
Banet-Weiser, Sarah, Roopali Mukherjee, and Gray Herman. 2019. 'Introduction - Postrace Projects'. In *Racism Postrace*, edited by Roopali Mukherjee, Sarah Banet-Weiser, and Herman Gray, 1–24. Durham, NC: Duke University Press.
Bartlett, Jamie, Jeremy Reffin, Noelle Rumball, and Sarah Williamson. 2014. 'Anti-Social Media'. Demos. https://www.demos.co.uk/files/DEMOS_Anti-social_Media.pdf?1391774638.
Bar-Yam, Yaneer. 2011. 'Concepts: Power Law'. New England Complex Systems Institute. https://necsi.edu/power-law.
Beauchamp, Zack. 2019. 'The Extremist Philosophy That's More Violent than the Alt-Right and Growing in Popularity'. Vox. 11 November 2019. https://www.vox.com/the-highlight/2019/11/11/20882005/accelerationism-white-supremacy-christchurch.
Bender, Emily M., Timnit Gebru, Angelina McMillan-Major, and Margaret Mitchell. 2021. 'On the Dangers of Stochastic Parrots: Can Language Models Be Too Big?' In *Proceedings of the 2021 ACM Conference on Fairness, Accountability, and Transparency*, 610–23. FAccT '21. New York: Association for Computing Machinery. https://doi.org/10.1145/3442188.3445922.
Benjamin, Ruha. 2016. 'Racial Fictions, Biological Facts: Expanding the Sociological Imagination Through Speculative Methods'. *Catalyst: Feminism, Theory, Technoscience* 2 (2): 1–28. https://doi.org/10.28968/cftt.v2i2.28798.

———. 2019. *Race After Technology*. London: Polity.

———. 2020. 'Reimagining the Default Settings of Technology & Society'. In *ICLR: 2020 Vision*. https://iclr.cc/virtual_2020/speaker_3.html.

Berry, Jeffrey M., and Sarah Sobieraj. 2014. *The Outrage Industry: Political Opinion Media and the New Incivility*. Studies in Postwar American Political Development. Oxford: Oxford University Press.

Bhatt, Chetan. 2021. 'White Extinction: Metaphysical Elements of Contemporary Western Fascism'. *Theory, Culture & Society* 38 (1): 27–52. https://doi.org/10.1177/0263276420925523.

Bijker, Wiebe E., Thomas Parke Hughes, and Trevor Pinch, eds. 2012. *The Social Construction of Technological Systems: New Directions in the Sociology and History of Technology*. Anniversary ed. Cambridge, MA: MIT Press.

Birhane, Abeba, Pratyusha Kalluri, Dallas Card, William Agnew, Ravit Dotan, and Michelle Bao. 2021. 'The Values Encoded in Machine Learning Research (Preprint)'. *ArXiv:2106.15590 [Cs]*, 1–28.

Bodley, John. 2003. *Why Scale Matter*. London: Routledge.

Bonilla, Yarimar, and Jonathan Rosa. 2015. '#Ferguson: Digital Protest, Hashtag Ethnography, and the Racial Politics of Social Media in the United States: #Ferguson'. *American Ethnologist* 42 (1): 4–17. https://doi.org/10.1111/amet.12112.

Bonilla-Silva, Eduardo. 2006. *Racism without Racists: Color-Blind Racism and the Persistence of Racial Inequality in the United States*. Rowman & Littlefield Publishers.

———. 2015. 'More than Prejudice: Restatement, Reflections, and New Directions in Critical Race Theory'. *Sociology of Race and Ethnicity* 1 (1): 75–89. https://doi.org/10.1177/2332649214557042.

Boomen, Marianne van den, Sybille Lammes, Ann-Sophie Lehmann, Joost Raessens, and Mirko Tobias Schäfer, eds. 2009. 'Introduction: From the Virtual to Matters of Fact and Concern'. In *Digital Material*, 7–18. Tracing New Media in Everyday Life and Technology. Amsterdam: Amsterdam University Press. https://www.jstor.org/stable/j.ctt46mxjv.3.

Borch, Christian. 2009. 'Body to Body: On the Political Anatomy of Crowds'. *Sociological Theory* 27 (3): 271–90.

Box, George E.P. 1976. 'Science and Statistics'. *Journal of the American Statistical Association* 71 (356): 791–99. https://doi.org/10.1080/01621459.1976.10480949.

boyd, danah, and Kate Crawford. 2012. 'CRITICAL QUESTIONS FOR BIG DATA: Provocations for a Cultural, Technological, and Scholarly Phenomenon'. *Information, Communication & Society* 15 (5): 662–79. https://doi.org/10.1080/1369118X.2012.678878.

Bray, Kirsten, and Christina Harrington. 2021. 'Speculative Blackness: Considering Afrofuturism in the Creation of Inclusive Speculative Design Probes'. In *Designing Interactive Systems Conference 2021*, 1793–1806. DIS '21. New York: Association for Computing Machinery. https://doi.org/10.1145/3461778.3462002.

Brighenti, Andrea Mubi. 2010. 'Tarde, Canetti, and Deleuze on Crowds and Packs'. *Journal of Classical Sociology* 10 (4): 291–314. https://doi.org/10.1177/1468795X10379675.

Brock, Jr. André. 2020. *Distributed Blackness: African American Cybercultures*. New York: NYU Press.

Brogden, Mike. 1987. 'The Emergence of the Police—the Colonial Dimension'. *The British Journal of Criminology* 27 (1): 4–14.

Broido, Anna D., and Aaron Clauset. 2019. 'Scale-Free Networks Are Rare'. *Nature Communications* 10 (1): 1017. https://doi.org/10.1038/s41467-019-08746-5.

Brown, Wendy. 2017. 'Apocalyptic Populism'. *Eurozine*, 1–11.

Browne, Simone. 2015. *Dark Matters: On the Surveillance of Blackness*. Durham, NC: Duke University Press.

Bucher, Taina. 2012. 'A Technicity of Attention: How Software "makes Sense"'. *Culture Machine* 13. https://culturemachine.net/wp-content/uploads/2019/01/470 -993-1-PB.pdf.

———. 2018. *If...Then: Algorithmic Power and Politics*. Oxford Studies in Digital Politics. Oxford, New York: Oxford University Press.

Carr, Nicholas. 2010. '"It's Not a Bug, It's a Feature." Trite—or Just Right?' *Wired*. https://www.wired.com/story/its-not-a-bug-its-a-feature/.

Castelvecchi, Davide. 2020. 'Mathematicians Urge Colleagues to Boycott Police Work in Wake of Killings'. *Nature*, June. https://doi.org/10.1038/d41586-020 -01874-9.

Certeau, Michel de. 1984. *The Practice of Everyday Life*. University of California Press.

Chan, Elizabeth. 2016. 'Donald Trump, Pepe the Frog, and White Supremacists: An Explainer'. Hillary for America. 2016. https://web.archive.org/web /20160913005513/https://www.hillaryclinton.com/feed/donald-trump-pepe-the -frog-and-white-supremacists-an-explainer/.

Chun, Wendy Hui Kyong. 2013. *Programmed Visions: Software and Memory*. Cambridge, MA: MIT Press.

———. 2015. 'Networks NOW: Belated Too Early'. *Amerikastudien / American Studies* 60 (1): 37–58.

———. 2019. 'Queerying Homophily'. In *Pattern Discrimination*, edited by Clemens Apprich, Wendy Hui Kyong Chun, Florian Cramer, and Hito Steyerl, 59–98. University of Minnesota Press.

———. 2021. *Discriminating Data: Correlation, Neighborhoods, and the New Politics of Recognition*. Cambridge, MA: The MIT Press.

Citarella, Joshua. 2021. 'There's a New Tactic for Exposing You to Radical Content Online: The "Slow Red-Pill"'. *The Guardian*, 15 July 2021, sec. Opinion. https:// www.theguardian.com/commentisfree/2021/jul/15/theres-a-new-tactic-for-expos-ing-you-to-radical-content-online-the-slow-red-pill.

Citton, Yves. 2017. *The Ecology of Attention*. English edition. Cambridge: Polity.

Clayton, Aubrey. 2020. 'How Eugenics Shaped Statistics'. Nautilus. 28 October 2020. http://nautil.us/issue/92/frontiers/how-eugenics-shaped-statistics.

Clough, Patricia Ticineto, Karen Gregory, Benjamin Haber, and R. Joshua Scannell. 2015. 'The Datalogical Turn'. In *Non-Representational Methodologies: Re-Envisioning Research*, edited by Phillip Vannini, 146–64. London: Routledge.

Cottom, Tressie McMillan. 2014. 'Racists Getting Fired: The Sins of Whiteness on Social Media'. Tressie McMillan Cottom. 2 December 2014. https://tressiemc.com /uncategorized/racists-getting-fired-the-sins-of-whiteness-on-social-media/.

Coughlan, Sean. 2020. 'A-Levels and GCSEs: Boris Johnson Blames "Mutant Algorithm" for Exam Fiasco'. *BBC News*. https://www.bbc.com/news/education -53923279.

Couldry, Nick, and Ulises A. Mejias. 2018. 'Data Colonialism: Rethinking Big Data's Relation to the Contemporary Subject'. *Television & New Media* 20 (4): 1–14. https://doi.org/10.1177/1527476418796632.

———. 2019. *The Costs of Connection: How Data Is Colonizing Human Life and Appropriating It for Capitalism*. Stanford, CA: Stanford University Press.

Covington, Paul, Jay Adams, and Emre Sargin. 2016. 'Deep Neural Networks for YouTube Recommendations'. In *Proceedings of the 10th ACM Conference on Recommender Systems*, 191–98. Boston, MA: ACM. https://doi.org/10.1145/2959100 .2959190.

Daniels, Jessie. 2009. *Cyber Racism: White Supremacy Online and the New Attack on Civil Rights*. Lanham, MD: Rowman & Littlefield Publishers.

———. 2018. 'The Algorithmic Rise of the "Alt-Right"'. *Contexts* 17 (1): 60–65. https://doi.org/10.1177/1536504218766547.

Danks, David, and Alex John London. 2017. 'Algorithmic Bias in Autonomous Systems'. In *Proceedings of the Twenty-Sixth International Joint Conference on Artificial Intelligence*, 4691–97. Melbourne: International Joint Conferences on Artificial Intelligence Organization. https://doi.org/10.24963/ijcai.2017/654.

Davey, Jacob, and Julia Ebner. 2019. 'The "Great Replacement": The Violent Consequences of Mainstreamed Extremism'. London: Institute for Strategic Dialogue. https://www.isdglobal.org/isd-publications/the-great-replacement-the-violent-con-sequences-of-mainstreamed-extremism/.

Davies, Thom. 2022. 'Slow Violence and Toxic Geographies: "Out of Sight" to Whom?' *Environment and Planning C: Politics and Space* 40 (2): 409–27. https:// doi.org/10.1177/2399654419841063.

Davies, William. 2018. *Nervous States: How Feeling Took Over the World*. London: Random House.

Dean, Jodi. 2010. *Blog Theory*. Cambridge, MA: Polity.

Debord, Guy. 1967. *Society of the Spectacle*. Bread and Circuses Publishing.

DeLanda, Manuel. 2016. *Assemblage Theory*. Edinburgh: Edinburgh University Press.

Deleuze, Gilles. 1992. 'Postscript on the Societies of Control'. *October* 59: 3–7.

———. 2006. *Two Regimes of Madness: Texts and Interviews 1975–1995*. Los Angeles: Semiotext(e).

Deleuze, Gilles, and Félix Guattari. 1987. *A Thousand Plateaus: Capitalism and Schizophrenia*. Minneapolis, MN: University of Minnesota Press.

Delgado, Richard, and Jean Stefancic. 2017. *Critical Race Theory: An Introduction*. Critical America. New York: New York University Press.

Dennis Jr., David. 2021. 'A Poet and a Protester, Gil Scott-Heron Captured His Time — and Ours'. https://andscape.com/features/a-poet-and-a-protester-gil-scott-heron -captured-his-time-and-ours/.

Dery, Mark. 1994. 'Black to the Future: Interviews with Samuel R. Delany, Greg Tate, and Tricia Rose'. In *Black to the Future: Interviews with Samuel R. Delany, Greg Tate, and Tricia Rose*, 179–222. Duke University Press. https://doi.org/10.1515/9780822396765-010.

Dhrodia, Azmina. 2018. 'Unsocial Media: A Toxic Place for Women'. *IPPR Progressive Review* 24 (4): 381–87.

D'Ignazio, Catherine, and Lauren Klein. 2020. *Data Feminism*. Cambridge, MA: MIT Press.

Dijck, José van. 2013. *The Culture of Connectivity: A Critical History of Social Media*. Oxford: Oxford University Press.

Doctorow, Cory. 2019. 'Barlow's Legacy'. *Duke Law & Technology Review* 18 (1): 61–68.

Dongus, Ariana. 2019. 'Galton's Utopia – Data Accumulation in Biometric Capitalism'. http://spheres-journal.org/galtons-utopia-data-accumulation-in-biometric-capitalism/.

Donovan, Joan, Becca Lewis, and Brian Friedberg. 2018. 'Parallel Ports. Sociotechnical Change from the Alt-Right to Alt-Tech'. In *Post-Digital Cultures of the Far Right*, edited by Maik Fielitz and Nick Thurston, 49–66. Bielefeld: Transcript Verlag. https://doi.org/10.14361/9783839446706-004.

Dourish, Paul. 2016. 'Algorithms and Their Others: Algorithmic Culture in Context'. *Big Data & Society* 3 (2): 1–11. https://doi.org/10.1177/2053951716665128.

Easley, David, and Jon Kleinberg. 2010. *Networks, Crowds, and Markets: Reasoning About a Highly Connected World*. Cambridge: Cambridge University Press. https://www.cs.cornell.edu/home/kleinber/networks-book/.

Ebner, Julia, Maik Fielitz, and Nick Thurston. 2019. 'Innovative Ways to Counter Far-Right Communication Tactics'. In *Post-Digital Cultures of the Far Right*, 71: 169–82. Political Science. Leipzig: Deutsche Nationalbibliothek.

Eno, Brian. 1978. 'Music for Airports Liner Notes'. http://music.hyperreal.org/artists/brian_eno/MFA-txt.html.

Escobar, Arturo. 2007. 'The "ontological Turn" in Social Theory. A Commentary on "Human Geography without Scale", by Sallie Marston, John Paul Jones II and Keith Woodward'. *Transactions of the Institute of British Geographers* 32 (1): 106–11. https://doi.org/10.1111/j.1475-5661.2007.00243.x.

Essed, Philomena. 1991. *Understanding Everyday Racism: An Interdisciplinary Theory*. London: Sage.

Eubanks, Virginia. 2018. *Automating Inequality: How High-Tech Tools Profile, Police, and Punish the Poor*. London: St. Martin's Press.

Evans, Brad. 2013. 'Fascism and the Bio-Political'. In *Deleuze & Fascism: Security: War: Aesthetics*, edited by Julian Reid and Brad Evans, 42–63. London: Routledge.

Evans, Brad, and Julian Reid. 2013. 'Introduction: Fascism in All Its Forms'. In *Deleuze & Fascism: Security: War: Aesthetics*, edited by Julian Reid and Brad Evans, 1–12. London: Routledge.

Fielitz, Maik, and Nick Thurston, eds. 2019. *Post-Digital Cultures of the Far Right: Online Actions and Offline Consequences in Europe and the US*. 1. Auflage. Political Science, Volume 71. Bielefeld: Transcript.

Flowers, Johnathon. 2022. 'The Whiteness of Mastodon'. Tech Policy Press. 23 November 2022. https://techpolicy.press/the-whiteness-of-mastodon/.

Foucault, Michel. 1977. *Discipline and Punish: The Birth of the Prison*. London: Vintage Books.

———. 2003. *Abnormal: Lectures at the Collège de France 1974–1975*. London: Verso.

———. 2004. *Society Must Be Defended: Lectures at the Collège de France, 1975–76*. London: Penguin.

———. 2007. *Security, Territory, Population: Lectures at the Collège de France, 1977–78*. Basingstoke: Palgrave Macmillan.

Fox, Nick J., and Pam Alldred. 2015. 'New Materialist Social Inquiry: Designs, Methods and the Research-Assemblage'. *International Journal of Social Research Methodology* 18 (4): 399–414. https://doi.org/10.1080/13645579.2014.921458.

Franklin, Seb. 2018. 'Periodising (with) Control'. In *Control Culture: Foucault and Deleuze After Discipline*, edited by Frida Beckman. 44–62. Edinburgh: Edinburgh University Press.

Fuchs, Christian, and Klaus Unterberger, eds. 2021. *The Public Service Media and Public Service Internet Manifesto*. University of Westminster Press. https://doi.org/10.16997/book60.

Future of Life Institute. 2023. 'Pause Giant AI Experiments: An Open Letter'. *Future of Life Institute* (blog). https://futureoflife.org/open-letter/pause-giant-ai-experiments/.

Galloway, Alexander R. 2004. *Protocol: How Control Exists After Decentralization*. Leonardo. Cambridge, MA: MIT Press.

———. 2012. 'Black Box Black Bloc'. In *Communization and Its Discontents: Contestation, Critique, and Contemporary Struggles*, edited by Benjamin Noys. Minor Compositions. 237–249. Wivenhoe New York Port Watson: Minor Compositions.

Gambetti, Zeynep. 2018. 'How "Alternative" Is the Alt-Right?' *Praxis 13/13*. http://blogs.law.columbia.edu/praxis1313/zeynep-gambetti-how-alternative-is-the-alt-right/?cn-reloaded=1.

Ganesh, Bharath. 2020. 'Weaponizing White Thymos: Flows of Rage in the Online Audiences of the Alt-Right'. *Cultural Studies*, January, 1–33. https://doi.org/10.1080/09502386.2020.1714687.

Ganesh, Maya Indira. 2018. 'The Center for Humane Technology Doesn't Want Your Attention - Cyborgology'. https://thesocietypages.org/cyborgology/2018/02/09/the-center-for-humane-technology-doesnt-want-your-attention/.

Gebru, Timnit (@timntGebru). 2020b. 'Even Amidst of World Wide Protests People Don't Hear Our Voices'. Twitter. https://twitter.com/timnitGebru/status/1274809418475950080.

———. 2020a. 'I'm Sick of This Framing. Tired of It'. Twitter. https://twitter.com/timnitGebru/status/1274809417653866496.

Genosko, Gary. 2017. 'Black Holes of Politics: Resonances of Microfascism'. *La Deleuziana – Online Journal of Philosophy* 5: 59–67.

Gillespie, Tarleton. 2018. *Custodians of the Internet: Platforms, Content Moderation, and the Hidden Decisions That Shape Social Media*. London: Yale University Press.

Gilmore, Ruth Wilson. 2007. *Golden Gulag: Prisons, Surplus, Crisis, and Opposition in Globalizing California*. Berkeley, CA: University of California Press.

———. 2022. *Abolition Geography: Essays Towards Liberation*. London: Verso Books.

Gilroy, Paul. 1987. *There Ain't No Black in the Union Jack*. London: Routledge.

Ging, Debbie, and Eugenia Siapera. 2018. 'Special Issue on Online Misogyny'. *Feminist Media Studies* 18 (4): 515–24. https://doi.org/10.1080/14680777.2018.1447345.

Giroux, Henry A. 2007. 'Violence, Katrina, and the Biopolitics of Disposability'. *Theory, Culture & Society* 24 (7–8): 305–9. https://doi.org/10.1177/02632764070240072510.

Goldacre, Ben. 2009. 'Datamining for Terrorists Would Be Lovely If It Worked – Bad Science'. http://www.badscience.net/2009/02/datamining-would-be-lovely-if-it-worked/.

Goldberg, David Theo. 1997. *Racial Subjects: Writing on Race in America*. London: Routledge.

———. 2015. *Are We All Postracial Yet?* London: Polity Press.

Gorwa, Robert, Reuben Binns, and Christian Katzenbach. 2020. 'Algorithmic Content Moderation: Technical and Political Challenges in the Automation of Platform Governance'. *Big Data & Society* 7 (1): 2053951719897945. https://doi.org/10.1177/2053951719897945.

Grandinetti, Justin, and Jeffrey Bruinsma. 2022. 'The Affective Algorithms of Conspiracy TikTok'. *Journal of Broadcasting & Electronic Media*, November, 1–20. https://doi.org/10.1080/08838151.2022.2140806.

Gray, Catriona. 2021. 'Data Dispossession'. *The Sociological Review Magazine*. https://doi.org/10.51428/tsr.ilzc1791.

Gray, Herman. 2019. 'Race After Race'. In *Racism Post Race*, edited by Roopali Mukherjee, Sarah Banet-Weiser, and Herman Gray, 23–36. Durham: Duke University Press.

'Greater Internet Fuckwad Theory'. 2012. 'Know Your Meme'. 12 June. https://knowyourmeme.com/memes/greater-internet-fuckwad-theory.

Guterres, António. 20121. 'What Is Hate Speech?' United Nations. https://www.un.org/en/hate-speech/understanding-hate-speech/what-is-hate-speech.

Hacking, Ian. 1990. *The Taming of Chance*. 1st edition. Cambridge; New York: Cambridge University Press.

Haines, Tom S.F. 2020. 'Thaines.Com - A-Levels: The Model Is Not the Student'. https://thaines.com/post/alevels2020.

Hall, Stuart. 1991. 'Old and New Identities, Old and New Ethnicities'. In *Culture, Globalization and the World System: Contemporary Conditions for the Representation of Identity*, edited by Anthony D. King. 41–68. Minneapolis, MN: University of Minnesota Press.

———. 1996. *Race: The Floating Signifier*. Classroom ed. Northampton, MA: Media Education Foundation.

Hanna, Alex, Emily Denton, Andrew Smart, and Jamila Smith-Loud. 2020. 'Towards a Critical Race Methodology in Algorithmic Fairness'. *Proceedings of the 2020*

Conference on Fairness, Accountability, and Transparency, 501–12. https://doi .org/10.1145/3351095.3372826.

Hardt, Michael, and Antonio Negri. 2000. *Empire*. Cambridge, MA: Harvard University Press.

Harry, Sydette. 2014. 'Attacking the Stream'. *Dissent Magazine*. https://www.dis-sentmagazine.org/online_articles/attacking-the-stream.

Harvey, David. 2007. *A Brief History of Neoliberalism*. Oxford University Press.

Hawley, George. 2017. *Making Sense of the Alt-Right*. New York: Columbia University Press.

Heidelberg Laureate Forum. n.d. 'ACM A.M. Turing Award'. Heidelberg Laureate Forum. Accessed 16 February 2022. https://www.heidelberg-laureate-forum.org/laureates/awards/acm-am-turing-award.html.

Hermansson, Patrik, David Lawrence, Joe Mulhall, and Simon Murdoch. 2020. *The International Alt-Right: Fascism for the 21st Century?* New York: Routledge.

Herod, Andrew. 2011. *Scale*. Key Ideas in Geography. London: Routledge.

Heynen, Robert, and Emily van der Meulen, eds. 2019. *Making Surveillance States: Transnational Histories*. London: University of Toronto Press.

Hong, Sun-ha. 2022. 'Predictions Without Futures'. *History and Theory*, 1–20. https://doi.org/10.1111/hith.12269.

Hook, Derek. 2005. 'Affecting Whiteness: Racism as Technology of Affect'. London: *LSE Research Online*, 74–99.

HOPE not Hate. 2022. 'State of HATE 2022: On the March Again'. *HOPE Not Hate* (blog). 9 March 2022. https://hopenothate.org.uk/2022/03/09/state-of-hate-2022 -on-the-march-again/.

Horton, Zachary K. 2021. *The Cosmic Zoom: Scale, Knowledge, and Mediation*. Chicago, IL: The University of Chicago Press.

Hu, Tung-Hui. 2015. *A Prehistory of the Cloud*. Cambridge, MA: The MIT Press.

Huey, Laura, Joseph Varanese, and Ryan Broll. 2015. 'The Grey Sygnet Problem in Terrorism Research'. In *Social Networks, Terrorism and Counter-Terrorism: Radical and Connected*, edited by Martin Bouchard, 34–47. Routledge.

Hughey, Matthew W., and Jessie Daniels. 2013. 'Racist Comments at Online News Sites: A Methodological Dilemma for Discourse Analysis'. *Media, Culture & Society* 35 (3): 332–47. https://doi.org/10.1177/0163443712472089.

Hui, Yuk. 2016. *On the Existence of Digital Objects*. Minneapolis, MN: University of Minnesota Press.

Jones, Kristen P., Chad I. Peddie, Veronica L. Gilrane, Eden B. King, and Alexis L. Gray. 2016. 'Not So Subtle: A Meta-Analytic Investigation of the Correlates of Subtle and Overt Discrimination'. *Journal of Management* 42 (6): 1588–1613. https://doi.org/10.1177/0149206313506466.

Kafer, Gary. 2019. 'Surveillance Capitalism and Its Racial Discontents'. Jump Cut. http://ejumpcut.org/archive/jc59.2019/Kafer-Zuboff/index.html.

Kalluri, Pratyusha. 2020. 'Don't Ask If Artificial Intelligence Is Good or Fair, Ask How It Shifts Power'. *Nature* 583 (7815): 169. https://doi.org/10.1038/d41586-020 -02003-2.

Kapoor, Sayash, and Arvind Narayanan. 2022. 'AI Snake Oil'. Substack. https://
aisnakeoil.substack.com/.

Karp, Paul. 2018. '"OK to Be White":Australian Government Senators Condemn
"Anti-White Racism"'. *The Guardian*.https://www.theguardian.com/australia
-news/2018/oct/15/ok-to-be-white-australian-government-senators-condemn-anti
-white-racism.\sx

Katz, Yarden. 2020. *Artificial Whiteness: Politics and Ideology in Artificial Intelligence*. New York: Columbia University Press.

Keefe, Patrick Radden. 2006. 'Can Network Theory Thwart Terrorists?' *The New
York Times*, 12 March. https://www.nytimes.com/2006/03/12/magazine/can-net-
work-theory-thwart-terrorists.html.

Kellner, Douglas. 2017. 'Preface: Guy Debord, Donald Trump, and the Politics of
the Spectacle'. In *The Spectacle 2.0: Reading Debord in the Context of Digital
Capitalism*, edited by Marco Briziarelli and Emiliana Armano. London: University
of Westminster Press. https://doi.org/10.16997/book11.

King, Jamila. 2015. '#blacklivesmatter'. *The California Sunday Magazine*. 11
December 2015. https://story.californiasunday.com/black-lives-matter.

Kizilcec, René F., and Hansol Lee. 2021. 'Algorithmic Fairness in Education'. arXiv.
https://doi.org/10.48550/arXiv.2007.05443.

Koepnick, Lutz P. 1999. 'Fascist Aesthetics Revisited'. *Modernism/Modernity* 6 (1):
51–73. https://doi.org/10.1353/mod.1999.0009.

Köhler, Bernard, Sabrina David, and Jörg Blumtritt. 2010. 'The Slow Media Manifesto'. https://en.slow-media.net/manifesto.

Kolko, Beth E., Lisa Nakamura, and Gilbert B. Rodman, eds. 2000. *Race in Cyberspace*. New York: Routledge.

Krebs, Valdis. 2002. 'Uncloaking Terrorist Networks'. *First Monday* 7 (4). https://
doi.org/10.5210/fm.v7i4.941.

Kucharski, Adam. 2020. *The Rules of Contagion: Why Things Spread - and Why They
Stop*. Main edition. London: Wellcome Collection.

Kwet, Michael. 2019. 'Digital Colonialism: US Empire and the New Imperial-
ism in the Global South'. *Race & Class* 60 (4): 3–26. https://doi.org/10.1177
/0306396818823172.

Ladyman, James, James Lambert, and Karoline Wiesner. 2013. 'What Is a Complex
System?' *European Journal for Philosophy of Science* 3 (1): 33–67. https://doi.org
/10.1007/s13194-012-0056-8.

LeCun, Yann. 2020b. 'I Really Wish People of Good Will Who Have a Desire to
Address the Issue of Bias and Ethics in AI'. Facebook. https://www.facebook.com
/yann.lecun/posts/pfbid02MbM57YVbxtoD95wRdRs1wNWA4ayzQSPmRxfe
iRQ8aQwvwUzzpAcjJXG9L1PHmU5Xl.

LeCun, Yann (@ylecun). 2020b. 'ML Systems Are Biased When Data Is Biased'.
Twitter. https://twitter.com/ylecun/status/1274782757907030016?s=20&t=Guz-
wS6ERGNKn-ySm-WWDcQ.

Lee, Francis. 2021. 'Enacting the Pandemic: Analyzing Agency, Opacity, and Power
in Algorithmic Assemblages'. *Science & Technology Studies* 34 (1): 65–90. https://
doi.org/10.23987/sts.75323.

Lee, Francis, Jess Bier, Jeffrey Christensen, Lukas Engelmann, Claes-Fredrik Helgesson, and Robin Williams. 2019. 'Algorithms as Folding: Reframing the Analytical Focus'. *Big Data & Society* 6 (2): 205395171986381. https://doi.org/10.1177/2053951719863819.

Lentin, Alana. 2005. 'Replacing "Race", Historicizing "Culture" in Multiculturalism'. *Patterns of Prejudice* 39 (4): 379–96. https://doi.org/10.1080/00313220500347832.

———. 2016. 'Racism in Public or Public Racism: Doing Anti-Racism in "Post-Racial" Times'. *Ethnic and Racial Studies* 39 (1): 33–48. https://doi.org/10.1080/01419870.2016.1096409.

Lorde, Audre. 1979. 'The Master's Tools Will Never Dismantle the Master's House'. In *Second Sex Conference*. New York.

Lovink, Geert. 2007. *Zero Comments: Blogging and Critical Internet Culture*. 1st edition. New York: Routledge.

———. 2012. 'What Is the Social in Social Media?'. *e-flux* #40 .

Macey, David. 2009. 'Rethinking Biopolitics, Race and Power in the Wake of Foucault'. *Theory, Culture & Society* 26 (6): 186–205. https://doi.org/10.1177/0263276409349278.

Mackay, Robin, and Armen Avanessian, eds. 2014. *#Accelerate: The Accelerationist Reader*. 2nd edition. Falmouth: Urbanomic.

Mackenzie, Adrian. 2015. 'The Production of Prediction: What Does Machine Learning Want?' *European Journal of Cultural Studies* 18 (4–5): 429–45. https://doi.org/10.1177/1367549415577384.

Madrigal, Alexis C. 2013. '2013: The Year "the Stream" Crested'. *The Atlantic*. 12 December 2013. https://www.theatlantic.com/technology/archive/2013/12/2013-the-year-the-stream-crested/282202/.

Marche, Stephen. 2013. 'There Are No Saints Online'. *Esquire*. 23 April 2013. http://www.esquire.com/no-saints-online-0513.

Marcy, Richard T. 2020. 'Leadership of Socio-Political Vanguards: A Review and Future Directions'. *The Leadership Quarterly* 31 (1): 1–12. https://doi.org/10.1016/j.leaqua.2019.101372.

Marres, Noortje. 2017. *Digital Sociology: The Reinvention of Social Research*. London: Polity.

Marwick, Alice, and Rebecca Lewis. 2017. 'Media Manipulation and Disinformation Online'. *Data & Society Research Institute*.

Massanari, Adrienne. 2017. '#Gamergate and The Fappening: How Reddit's Algorithm, Governance, and Culture Support Toxic Technocultures'. *New Media & Society* 19 (3): 329–46. https://doi.org/10.1177/1461444815608807.

Massumi, Brian. 1995. 'The Autonomy of Affect'. *Cultural Critique* 31: 83–109. https://doi.org/10.2307/1354446.

———. 2005. 'Fear (the Spectrum Said)'. *Positions: East Asia Cultures Critique* 13 (1): 31–48.

———. 2015. *Ontopower: War, Powers, and the State of Perception*. Durham, NC: Duke University Press.

Matamoros-Fernández, Ariadna. 2017. 'Platformed Racism: The Mediation and Circulation of an Australian Race-Based Controversy on Twitter, Facebook and

YouTube'. *Information, Communication & Society* 20 (6): 930–46. https://doi.org
/10.1080/1369118X.2017.1293130.

Matamoros-Fernández, Ariadna, and Johan Farkas. 2021. 'Racism, Hate Speech, and
Social Media: A Systematic Review and Critique'. *Television & New Media* 22 (2):
205–24. https://doi.org/10.1177/1527476420982230.

Mbembe, Achille. 2003. 'Necropolitics'. *Public Culture* 15 (1): 11–40.

McCullough, Malcolm. 2013. *Ambient Commons: Attention in the Age of Embodied
Information*. Cambridge, MA: The MIT Press.

McQuillan, Dan. 2022. *Resisting AI: An Anti-Fascist Approach to Artificial Intelligence*. Bristol: Bristol University Press.

McWhorter, Ladelle. 2009. *Racism and Sexual Oppression in Anglo-America: A
Genealogy*. Bloomington, IN: Indiana University Press.

Mehrabi, Ninareh, Fred Morstatter, Nripsuta Saxena, Kristina Lerman, and Aram
Galstyan. 2021. 'A Survey on Bias and Fairness in Machine Learning'. arXiv.
https://doi.org/10.48550/arXiv.1908.09635.

Mejias, Ulises A., and Nick Couldry. 2019. 'Datafication'. *Internet Policy Review* 8
(4): 1–8.

Mejias, Ulises Ali. 2013. *Off the Network: Disrupting the Digital World*. University
of Minnesota Press. https://doi.org/10.5749/minnesota/9780816678990.001.0001.

———. 2020. 'To Fight Data Colonialism, We Need a Non-Aligned Tech Movement'. *Aljazeera*. https://www.aljazeera.com/opinions/2020/9/8/to-fight-data-colo-
nialism-we-need-a-non-aligned-tech-movement.

Menon, Sachit, Alexandru Damian, Shijia Hu, Nikhil Ravi, and Cynthia Rudin.
2020. 'PULSE: Self-Supervised Photo Upsampling via Latent Space Exploration
of Generative Models'. *ArXiv:2003.03808 [Cs, Eess]*, July. http://arxiv.org/abs
/2003.03808.

Miranda, Luis de. 2013. 'Is A New Life Possible? Deleuze and the Lines'. *Deleuze
Studies* 7 (1): 106–52. https://doi.org/10.3366/dls.2013.0096.

Mishan, Ligaya. 2020. 'The Long and Tortured History of Cancel Culture'. *New
York Times*. https://web.archive.org/web/20201211104654/https://www.nytimes
.com/2020/12/03/t-magazine/cancel-culture-history.html.

Mitchell, Peta. 2012. *Contagious Metaphor*. London: Bloomsbury.

Mol, Annemarie, and John Law. 1994. 'Regions, Networks and Fluids: Anaemia and
Social Topology'. *Social Studies of Science* 24 (4): 641–71. https://doi.org/10.1177
/030631279402400402.

Mondon, Aurelien, and Antonia Vaughan. 2021. 'The Trump Presidency and Mainstreaming of Far-Right Politics'. *Gale* (blog). https://www.gale.com/intl/essays
/aurelien-mondon-antonia-vaughan-trump-presidency-mainstreaming-far-right
-politics.

Mondon, Aurelien, and Aaron Winter. 2017. 'Articulations of Islamophobia: From
the Extreme to the Mainstream?' *Ethnic and Racial Studies*, May, 1–29. https://doi
.org/10.1080/01419870.2017.1312008.

Moss, Emanuel, Rumman Chowdhury, BogdanaRakova, Sonja Schmer-Galunder,
Reuben Binns, and Andrew Smart. 2019 'MachineBehaviour Is Old Wine in New
Bottles'. *Nature* 574: 176–176. https://doi.org/10.1038/d41586-019-03002-8.

Morozov, Evgeny. 2014. *To Save Everything, Click Here: The Folly of Technological Solutionism*. New York: PublicAffairs.

Mumford, Densua. 2022. 'Data Colonialism: Compelling and Useful, but Whither Epistemes?' *Information, Communication & Society* 25 (10): 1511–16. https://doi.org/10.1080/1369118X.2021.1986103.

Munk, Timme Bisgaard. 2017. '100,000 False Positives for Every Real Terrorist: Why Anti-Terror Algorithms Don't Work'. *First Monday* 22 (9). http://firstmonday.org/ojs/index.php/fm/article/view/7126.

Munn, Luke. 2019. 'Alt-Right Pipeline: Individual Journeys to Extremism Online'. *First Monday* 24 (6). https://doi.org/10.5210/fm.v24i6.10108.

Murray, Joy. 2012. 'Cybernetic Principles of Learning'. In *Encyclopedia of the Sciences of Learning*, edited by Norbert M. Seel, 901–4. Boston, MA: Springer US. https://doi.org/10.1007/978-1-4419-1428-6_829.

Murthy, Dhiraj, and Sanjay Sharma. 2019. 'Visualizing YouTube's Comment Space: Online Hostility as a Networked Phenomena'. *New Media & Society* 21 (1): 191–213. https://doi.org/10.1177/1461444818792393.

Nachtwey, Oliver, and Timo Seidl. 2020. 'The Solutionist Ethic and the Spirit of Digital Capitalism'. Working Paper. SocArXiv Papers. https://doi.org/10.31235/osf.io/sgjzq.

Nagle, Angela. 2017. *Kill All Normies: The Online Culture Wars from Tumblr and 4chan to the Alt-Right and Trump*. Winchester: Zero Books.

Nakamura, Lisa. 2013. 'Glitch Racism: Networks as Actors within Vernacular Internet Theory'. *Culture Digitally* (blog). http://culturedigitally.org/2013/12/glitch-racism-networks-as-actors-within-vernacular-internet-theory/.

Nakamura, Lisa, Peter Chow-White, Lisa Nakamura, and Chow-White, eds. 2012. 'Introduction - Race and Digital Technology: Code, the Color Line, and the Information Society'. In *Race After the Internet*, 1–20. New York: Routledge.

Narayanan, Arvind. 2022. 'TikTok's Secret Sauce'. The Knight First Amendment Institute. http://knightcolumbia.org/blog/tiktoks-secret-sauce.

NATM. n.d. 'Non-Aligned Technologies Movement'. Accessed 10 December 2022.

NeurIPS. 2023. 'NeurIPS 2021 Paper Checklist Guidelines'. NeurIPS. https://neurips.cc/Conferences/2021/PaperInformation/PaperChecklist.

Nicas, Jack. 2018. 'How YouTube Drives People to the Internet's Darkest Corners'. *The Wall Street Journal*. https://www.wsj.com/articles/how-youtube-drives-viewers-to-the-internets-darkest-corners-1518020478.

Nixon, Rob. 2011. *Slow Violence and the Environmentalism of the Poor*. Cambridge, MA: Harvard University Press.

Noble, Safiya Umoja. 2018. *Algorithms of Oppression: How Search Engines Reinforce Racism*. New York: NYU Press.

Ntoutsi, Eirini, Pavlos Fafalios, Ujwal Gadiraju et al. 2020. 'Bias in Data-Driven Artificial Intelligence Systems—An Introductory Survey'. *WIREs Data Mining and Knowledge Discovery* 10 (3): 1–14. https://doi.org/10.1002/widm.1356.

O'Donovan et al., Caroline. 2019. 'We Followed YouTube's Recommendation Algorithm Down the Rabbit Hole'. *BuzzFeed News*. 2019. https://www.buzzfeednews.com/article/carolineodonovan/down-youtubes-recommendation-rabbithole.

O'Neil, Cathy. 2016. *Weapons of Math Destruction: How Big Data Increases Inequality and Threatens Democracy*. Penguin.

———. 2020. *Are Algorithms Racist?* Bloomberg Quicktake. https://www.youtube.com/watch?v=971CFnYrBgw.

Ornes, Stephen. 2023. 'The Unpredictable Abilities Emerging From Large AI Models'. *Quanta Magazine*. 16 March 2023. https://www.quantamagazine.org/the-unpredictable-abilities-emerging-from-large-ai-models-20230316/.

Pasquale, Frank. 2015. *The Black Box Society: The Secret Algorithms That Control Money and Information*. Cambridge, MA: Harvard University Press.

Pasquinelli, Matteo. 2017. 'Machines That Morph Logic: Neural Networks and the Distorted Automation of Intelligence as Statistical Inference'. *Glass - Bead*, no. Site 1: Logic Gate, the Politics of the Artifactual Mind: 17.

Penny Arcade. 2004. 'Green Blackboards (And Other Anomalies)'. https://www.penny-arcade.com/comic/2004/03/19/green-blackboards-and-other-anomalies.

Pettis, Ben. 2019. 'Pepe the Frog and Drake Approves: Variances in the Exploitability of Meme Genres'. Unpublished Paper, 1–33. . https://benpettis.com/writing/2019/4/10/pepe-the-frog-and-drake-approves-variances-in-the-exploitability-of-meme-genres.

Phillips, Whitney. 2018a. 'Our Information Systems Aren't Broken — They're Working as Intended'. *Nieman Lab* (blog). https://www.niemanlab.org/2018/12/our-information-systems-arent-broken-theyre-working-as-intended/.

———. 2018b. 'The Oxygen of Amplification'. *Data & Society Institute*.

Phillips, Whitney, and Ryan M. Milner. 2017. *The Ambivalent Internet: Mischief, Oddity, and Antagonism Online*. London: Wiley.

———. 2021. *You Are Here: A Field Guide for Navigating Polarized Speech Conspiracy Theories, and Our Polluted Media Landscape*. London: The MIT Press.

Poell, Thomas, David Nieborg, and José van Dijck. 2019. 'Platformisation'. *Internet Policy Review* 8 (4): 1–13.

Poletti, Therese, and Jeremy Owens. 2022. '$1.4 Trillion? Big Tech's Pandemic Year Produces Mind-Boggling Financial Results'. *MarketWatch*. https://www.marketwatch.com/story/1-4-trillion-big-techs-pandemic-year-produces-mind-boggling-financial-results-11644096594.

Puar, Jasbir K. 2007. *Terrorist Assemblages: Homonationalism in Queer Times*. Durham, NC: Duke University Press.

———. 2017. *The Right to Maim: Debility, Capacity, Disability*. Durham, NC: Duke University Press Books.

Quijano, Anibal, and Michael Ennis. 2000. 'Coloniality of Power, Eurocentrism, and Latin America'. *Nepantla: Viewsfrom South* 1, (3): 533–80.

Rauch, Rachel. 2012. *Slow Media: Why Slow Is Satisfying, Sustainable, and Smart*. New York: Academic.

Ray, Rashawn, Melissa Brown, Neil Fraistat, and Edward Summers. 2017. 'Ferguson and the Death of Michael Brown on Twitter: #BlackLivesMatter, #TCOT, and the Evolution of Collective Identities'. *Ethnic and Racial Studies* 40 (11): 1797–1813. https://doi.org/10.1080/01419870.2017.1335422.

Reta, Mary. 2021. 'Chauvin Trial Is Another Display of the Nonchalance toward Black Death'. *NBC News*. 5 April 2021. https://www.nbcnews.com/think/opinion/derek-chauvin-trial-another-media-spectacle-causes-trauma-rather-healing-ncna1263062.

Rheingold, Howard. 2000. *The Virtual Community: Homesteading on the Electronic Frontier*. Revised edition. Cambridge, MA: MIT Press.

Ribeiro, Manoel Horta, Raphael Ottoni, Robert West, Virgílio A.F. Almeida, and Wagner Meira. 2020. 'Auditing Radicalization Pathways on YouTube'. In *Proceedings of the 2020 Conference on Fairness, Accountability, and Transparency*, 131–41. FAT* '20. New York: Association for Computing Machinery. https://doi.org/10.1145/3351095.3372879.

Rogers, Richard. 2013. *Digital Methods*. London: MIT. https://doi.org/10.7551/mitpress/8718.001.0001.

Saldanha, Arun. 2007. *Psychedelic White : Goa Trance and the Viscosity of Race*. University of Minnesota Press.

Sandset, Tony. 2021. 'The Necropolitics of COVID-19: Race, Class and Slow Death in an Ongoing Pandemic'. *Global Public Health* 16 (8–9): 1411–23. https://doi.org/10.1080/17441692.2021.1906927.

Sayyid, S., and Barnor Hesse. 2006. 'Narrating the Postcolonial Political and the Immigrant Imaginary'. In *A Postcolonial People: South Asians in Britain*, edited by N. Ali and V.S. Kalra, 13–31. London: C Hurst & Co Publishers Ltd.

Scannell, R. Joshua. 2019. 'This Is Not Minority Report: Predictive Policing and Population Racism'. In *Captivating Technology: Race, Carceral Technoscience, and Liberatory Imagination in Everyday Life*, edited by Ruha Benjamin, 107–29. Durham, NC: Duke University Press.

Schmidt, Eric, Jared Cohen, and Roger Wayne. 2014. *The New Digital Age: Reshaping the Future of People, Nations and Business*. Unabridged edition. Grand Haven, MI: Brilliance Audio.

Schonfeld, Eric. 2013. 'Jump Into the Stream'. *Esquire*. http://www.esquire.com/news-politics/a22310/no-saints-online-0513/.

Segura, María Soledad, and Silvio Waisbord. 2019. 'Between Data Capitalism and Data Citizenship'. *Television & New Media* 20 (4): 412–19. https://doi.org/10.1177/1527476419834519.

Sengoopta, Chandak. 2003. *Imprint of the Raj: How Fingerprinting Was Born in Colonial India*. 1st Edition. London: Macmillan.

SensorTower. 2020. 'The Top Mobile Apps, Games, and Publishers of 2020'. https://sensortower.com/blog/q4-2020-data-digest.

Sexton, Jared. 2015. 'Unbearable Blackness'. *Cultural Critique* 90: 159–78. https://doi.org/10.5749/culturalcritique.90.2015.0159.

Seymour, Richard. 2019. *The Twittering Machine*. London: The Indigo Press.

Shapiro, Aaron. 2017. 'Reform Predictive Policing'. *Nature* 541 (7638): 458–60. https://doi.org/10.1038/541458a.

———. 2019. 'Predictive Policing for Reform? Indeterminacy and Intervention in Big Data Policing'. *Surveillance & Society* 17 (3/4): 456–72. https://doi.org/10.24908/ss.v17i3/4.10410.

Sharma, Ashwani, and Sanjay Sharma. 2012. 'Editorial: Post-Racial Imaginaries – Connecting the Pieces'. *Darkmatter Journal* 9(1). https://web.archive.org/web /20210227133329/http://www.darkmatter101.org/site/2012/07/02/editorial-post -racial-imaginaries-connecting-the-pieces/.

Sharma, Sanjay. 2013. 'Black Twitter? Racial Hashtags, Networks and Contagion'. *New Formations* 78: 46–64.

Sharma, Sanjay, and Phillip Brooker. 2016. '#notracist: Exploring Racism Denial Talk on Twitter'. In *Digital Sociologies*, edited by Jessie Daniels, Karen Gregory, and Tressie McMillan Cottom, 459–81. Policy Press.

Sharma, Sanjay, and Jasbinder Nijjar. 2018. 'The Racialized Surveillant Assemblage: Islam and the Fear of Terrorism'. *Popular Communication* 16 (1): 72–85. https:// doi.org/10.1080/15405702.2017.1412441.

———. 2023. 'Post-Racial Politics, Pre-emption and in/Security'. *European Journal of Cultural Studies*. https://doi.org/10.1177/13675494231168177.

Sharma, Sanjay, and Ashwani Sharma. 2003. 'White Paranoia: Orientalism in the Age of Empire'. *Fashion Theory* 7 (3–4): 301–17.

Shepherd, Tamara, Alison Harvey, Tim Jordan, Sam Srauy, and Kate Miltner. 2015. 'Histories of Hating'. *Social Media + Society* 1 (2): 1–10. https://doi.org/10.1177 /2056305115603997.

Shirky, Clay. 2003. 'Power Laws, Weblogs, and Inequality'. http://www.shirky.com /writings/herecomeseverybody/powerlaw_weblog.html.

Shohat, Ella, and Robert Stam. 1994a. *Unthinking Eurocentrism: Multiculturalism and the Media*. Vol. Sightlines. London: Routledge.

———. 1994b. *Unthinking Eurocentrism: Multiculturalism and the Media*. Vol. Sightlines. London: Routledge.

Shomura, Chad. 2017. 'Exploring the Promise of New Materialisms'. *Lateral* 6 (1). https://doi.org/10.25158/L6.1.10.

ShotSpotter. n.d. 'Resource Management'. ShotSpotter. Accessed 11 August 2022. https://www.soundthinking.com/law-enforcement/resource-deployment -resourcerouter/.

Siapera, Eugenia. 2019. 'Organised and Ambient Digital Racism: Multidirectional Flows in the Irish Digital Sphere'. *Open Library of Humanities* 5 (1). https://doi .org/10.16995/olh.405.

Srinivasa, Srinath. 2018. *The Power Law of Information*. Delhi: Response Books. https://us.sagepub.com/en-us/nam/the-power-law-of-information/book230649.

Srnicek, Nick. 2016. *Platform Capitalism*. London: Polity.

Stage, Carsten. 2013. 'The Online Crowd: A Contradiction in Terms? On the Potentials of Gustave Le Bon's Crowd Psychology in an Analysis of Affective Blogging'. *Distinktion: Journal of Social Theory* 14 (2): 211–26. https://doi.org/10 .1080/1600910X.2013.773261.

Star, Merlin J. 2023. 'Mastodon and Defederation'. *Medium* (blog). 5 February 2023. https://medium.com/@merlinstar/mastodon-and-defederation-d2ab740e96bf.

Stark, Luke. 2019. 'Facial Recognition Is the Plutonium of AI'. *XRDS* 25 (3): 50–55. https://doi.org/10.1145/3313129.

Stockford, Ian. 2020. 'Awarding GCSE, AS, A Level, Advanced Extension Awards and Extended Project Qualifications in Summer 2020: Interim Report'. OFqual.

Stokes, Jon. 2021. 'Understanding the Role of "Racist Algorithms" in AI Ethics Discourse'. https://doxa.substack.com/p/understanding-the-role-of-racist.

Stoler, Ann Laura. 1995. *Race and the Education of Desire: Foucault's History of Sexuality and the Colonial Order of Things*. 1st edition. Durham, NC: Duke University Press.

Strapagiel, Lauren. 2020. 'This Researcher's Observation Shows The Uncomfortable Bias Of TikTok's Algorithm'. *BuzzFeed News*. https://www.buzzfeednews.com/article/laurenstrapagiel/tiktok-algorithim-racial-bias.

Sue, Derald Wing. 2010. *Microaggressions in Everyday Life: Race, Gender, and Sexual Orientation*. 1st edition. Hoboken, NJ: Wiley.

Suresh, Harini, and John V. Guttag. 2021. 'A Framework for Understanding Sources of Harm throughout the Machine Learning Life Cycle'. *Equity and Access in Algorithms, Mechanisms, and Optimization*, October, 1–9. https://doi.org/10.1145/3465416.3483305.

Swanton, Dan. 2010. 'Sorting Bodies: Race, Affect, and Everyday Multiculture in a Mill Town in Northern England'. *Environment and Planning A* 42 (10): 2332–50. https://doi.org/10.1068/a42395.

Syed, Moin. 2021. 'The Logic of Microaggressions Assumes a Racist Society'. *Perspectives on Psychological Science* 16 (5): 926–31. https://doi.org/10.1177/1745691621994263.

Taleb, Nassim Nicholas. 2010. *The Black Swan: The Impact of the Highly Improbable*. 2nd edition. New York: Penguin.

Taylor, Chloë. 2011. 'Race and Racism in Foucault's Collège de France Lectures: Race and Racism'. *Philosophy Compass* 6 (11): 746–56. https://doi.org/10.1111/j.1747-9991.2011.00443.x.

Tennison, Jeni. 2020. 'How Does Ofqual's Grading Algorithm Work?' RPubs. https://rpubs.com/JeniT/ofqual-algorithm.

Terranova, Tiziana. 2004. *Network Culture: Politics for the Information Age*. London: Pluto Press.

Titley, Gavan. 2019. *Racism and Media*. London: SAGE.

Tomalin, Marcus. 2023. 'Rethinking Online Friction in the Information Society'. *Journal of Information Technology* 38 (1): 2–15. https://doi.org/10.1177/02683962211067812.

Topinka, Robert. 2019. 'Back to a Past That Was Futuristic: The Alt-Right and the Uncanny Form of Racism'. *B2o: An Online Journal*. https://www.boundary2.org/2019/10/robert-topinka-back-to-a-past-that-was-futuristic-the-alt-right-and-the-uncanny-form-of-racism/.

Tufekci, Zeynep. 2018. 'YouTube, the Great Radicalizer'. *The New York Times*. https://www.nytimes.com/2018/03/10/opinion/sunday/youtube-politics-radical.html.

Udupa, Sahana, and Ethiraj Gabriel Dattatreyan. 2023. *Digital Unsettling: Decoloniality and Dispossession in the Age of Social Media*. NYU Press.

United Nations. 2019. 'UN Strategy and Plan of Action on Hate Speech'. United Nations. https://www.un.org/en/genocideprevention/documents/UN%20Strategy

%20and%20Plan%20of%20Action%20on%20Hate%20Speech%2018%20June %20SYNOPSIS.pdf.

Valayden, Chandiren. 2013. *Outbreak Racism: The Embrace of Risk after Structural Racism*. Vol. PhD Thesis. University of California, Irvine.

Vila, Pablo, and Edward Avery-Natale. 2020. 'Towards an Affective Understanding of Processes of Racialization'. *Ethnicities* 20 (5): 844–62. https://doi.org/10.1177 /1468796820909453.

Vincent, James. 2019. '"Godfathers of AI" Honored with Turing Award, the Nobel Prize of Computing'. The Verge. 27 March 2019. https://www.theverge.com/2019 /3/27/18280665/ai-godfathers-turing-award-2018-yoshua-bengio-geoffrey-hinton -yann-lecun.

Von Hilgers, Philipp. 2011. 'The History of the Black Box: The Clash of a Thing and Its Concept'. *Cultural Politics: An International Journal* 7 (1): 41–58. https://doi .org/10.2752/175174311X12861940861707.

Vukov, Tamara. 2016. 'Target Practice'. *Transfers* 6 (1): 80–97. https://doi.org/10 .3167/TRANS.2016.060107.

Wang, Jackie. 2018. *Carceral Capitalism*. Semiotext(e) Intervention Series 21. South Pasadena, CA: Semiotext(e).

Weheliye, Alexander G. 2014. *Habeas Viscus: Racializing Assemblages, Biopolitics, and Black Feminist Theories of the Human*. Durham, NC: Duke University Press Books.

Weimann, Gabriel, and Natalie Masri. 2020. 'Research Note: Spreading Hate on TikTok'. *Studies in Conflict & Terrorism*, June, 1–14. https://doi.org/10.1080 /1057610X.2020.1780027.

Wendling, Mike. 2018. *Alt-Right: From 4chan to the White House*. London: Pluto Press.

White, Rachel Faulkner, Manoush Zomorodi, and Katie Simon. 2022. 'Yaël Eisenstat: Why We Need More Friction on Social Media'. *NPR*, 7 October 2022. https:// www.npr.org/2022/09/30/1127249176/yael-eisenstat-why-we-need-more-friction -on-social-media.

Williams, Matthew. 2021. *The Science of Hate: How Prejudice Becomes Hate and What We Can Do to Stop It*. London: Faber & Faber.

Wilson, Andrew. 2018. '#whitegenocide, the Alt-Right and Conspiracy Theory: How Secrecy and Suspicion Contributed to the Mainstreaming of Hate'. *Secrecy and Society* 1 (2): 1–46. https://doi.org/10.31979/2377-6188.2018.010201.

Wilson, Jason. 2018. '"It's OK to Be White" Is Not a Joke, It's Careless Politicians Helping the Far Right'. *The Guardian*. https://www.theguardian.com/comment-isfree/2018/oct/16/its-ok-to-be-white-is-not-a-joke-its-careless-politicians-helping -the-far-right.

Winner, Langdon. 1980. 'Do Artifacts Have Politics?' *Daedalus* 109 (1): 121–36. https://doi.org/10.4324/9781315259697.

Womack, Ytasha. 2013. *Afrofuturism: The World of Black Sci-Fi and Fantasy Culture*. Chicago: Chicago Review Press.

York, Jillian C., and Corynne McSherry. 2019. 'Content Moderation Is Broken: Let Us Count the Ways'. Electronic Frontier Foundation. 29 April 2019. https://www .eff.org/deeplinks/2019/04/content-moderation-broken-let-us-count-ways.

Zakrzewski, Cat, Joseph Menn, and Naomi Nix. 2022. 'Twitter Dissolves Trust and Safety Council'. *Washington Post*, 13 December 2022. https://www.washington-post.com/technology/2022/12/12/musk-twitter-harass-yoel-roth/.

Zappavigna, Michele. 2015. 'Searchable Talk: The Linguistic Functions of Hashtags'. *Social Semiotics* 25 (3): 274–91. https://doi.org/10.1080/10350330.2014.996948.

Zuboff, Shoshana. 2016. 'Google as a Fortune Teller: The Secrets of Surveillance Capitalism'. *Frankfurter Allgemeine*, sec. *Feuilleton*. https://www.faz.net/1 .4103616.

———. 2019. *The Age of Surveillance Capitalism: The Fight for a Human Future at the New Frontier of Power*. 1st edition. New York: Public Affairs.

Zulli, Diana, Miao Liu, and Robert Gehl. 2020. 'Rethinking the "Social" in "Social Media": Insights into Topology, Abstraction, and Scale on the Mastodon Social Network'. *New Media & Society* 22 (7): 1188–1205. https://doi.org/10.1177 /1461444820912533.

Zulli, Diana, and David James Zulli. 2022. 'Extending the Internet Meme: Conceptualizing Technological Mimesis and Imitation Publics on the TikTok Platform'. *New Media & Society* 24 (8): 1872–90. https://doi.org/10.1177/1461444820983603.

Index

About the Author

Sanjay Sharma works in the *Centre for Interdisciplinary Methodologies*, University of Warwick, UK. His research critically interrogates how existing and new forms of biopolitical control are constituted via digital technologies, media and culture. He has published widely on the intersections of race, technology and power, by grasping how race and racism are *emergent* digital phenomena, mutating through entanglements with networked relations, algorithmic profiling, datafication, platform architectures and economies. A materialist understanding of digital ecologies opens new possibilities for rethinking and resisting the contemporary force of racism and whiteness.

www.ingramcontent.com/pod-product-compliance
Lightning Source LLC
Chambersburg PA
CBHW022326280326
41932CB00010B/1241